Signs
and
Symbols
Around
the
World

Secret Script Picture by Paul Klee.

Signs and Symbols Around the World

Elizabeth S. Helfman

SIGNS AND SYMBOLS AROUND THE WORLD

iUniverse books may be ordered through booksellers or by contacting:

iUniverse
1663 Liberty Drive
Bloomington, IN 47403
www.iuniverse.com
844-349-9409

ISBN: 978-0-5951-2026-0 (sc)

Print information available on the last page.

iUniverse rev. date: 08/07/2020

To
LAVINIA DOBLER
good helper and good friend

Acknowledgments

It would be impossible to mention individually all the people who have helped with the preparation of this book. Special thanks are due, however, to Rudolph Modley, co-chairman with Margaret Mead of Glyphs, Incorporated; M. Esther Harding, M.D.; Soichi Kato of the International Committee for Breaking the Language Barrier, Inc.; and Mr. C. K. Bliss, inventor of Semantography, for his enthusiastic assistance.

I also wish to thank the following individuals and organizations for their cooperation in helping me to obtain illustrative materials for this book and/or their permission to reproduce copyrighted signs and symbols:

The American Society of Mechanical Engineers

Boise Cascade, for their copyrighted logo

Brookhaven National Laboratory

Brooklyn Bureau of Social Service and Children's Aid Society

The Chase Manhattan Bank

COSMOPRESS 1967, by French Reproduction Rights, Inc., for "Secret Script Picture" by Paul Klee

Deere & Company, Moline, Illinois

E. I. du Pont de Nemours & Company, Inc.

The Experiment in International Living

Icograda Commission on International Signs and Symbols, for the students' award-winning signs, Copyright ICOGRADA 1966

International Paper Company

ISIS—Mariano Comense (Italy), for the use of their trademark

Language Research, Inc., for the diagram from page 35 of *Basic English and Its Uses* by I. A. Richards. W. W. Norton, 1943

Los Alamos Scientific Laboratory, University of California

Robin Maugham, for the sign of Somerset Maugham

William Morrow & Company, Inc., for the signs from *Indian Picture Writing* by Robert Hofsinde. © 1959 by Robert Hofsinde

National Biscuit Company

Olivetti General Electric, for the proposed signs for operating computers

Philadelphia Museum of Art: The Louise and Walter Arensberg Collection, for "Circles in a Circle" by Wassily Kandinsky, 1923

Frederick A. Praeger, Inc., Publishers, for the prehistoric cave painting from *Art In the Ice Age* by Johannes Maringer and Hans-Georg Bandi. New York, 1953

Routledge & Kegan Paul Ltd., for ISOTYPES from *International Picture Language* by Otto Neurath, published by Kegan Paul, Trench, Trubner, 1936

Semantography (Blissymbolics) Publications, 2 Vicar St., Coogee 2934, Sydney, Australia.

The Twentieth Century Fund, for graphs from *USA and Its Economic Future*

United Nations World Health Organization

The United States Conference for the World Council of Churches, Inc.

United States Department of Agriculture, Federal Extension Service, for the 4-H Club name and emblem

United States Department of the Army, Office of Civil Defense, for the sign indicating Fallout Shelter

United States Department of Commerce, Environmental Science Services Administration, Weather Bureau

Acknowledgments / 9

United States of America Standards Institute

United States Olympic Committee

The Universal and International Exhibition of 1967,
Montreal, Canada, for its emblem, © Copyright 1963 Canadian
Corporation for the 1967 World Exhibition

Weyerhaeuser Company

Albert Whitman & Company, for logging signs from
From Tall Timber by Dirk Gringhuis

The Wool Bureau, Incorporated

World Wildlife Fund

Contents

Signs
and
Symbols
Around
the
World

1/

This
Book is
About
Signs and
Symbols

Signs are everywhere around you. Arrows tell you where to go or where to look. Commas and periods show you when to pause as you read. In mathematics, signs tell you to add or subtract or divide. Traffic signs help drivers to drive carefully and pedestrians to cross the street safely. Trademarks are signs that tell you what company made the crackers you buy or the carton your television set came in.

→ . , ; ? + ÷ ⊖ ⌖ 𝄞

None of the above signs depends on words. All of them can be understood by people who speak different languages —*if* they have learned what the signs mean. This book is about many of the signs and symbols that communicate facts and ideas, and sometimes feelings, to people throughout the world.

There are many ways of expressing ideas and feelings. You can express joy by laughing, unhappiness by weeping. You can gesture with your hands to help get your meaning across. You nod your head to say yes, and shake it sideways to say no. You can speak. But these expressions do not last. A moment later they are gone forever.

Words that are written or printed will last much longer. That is why books have had such a great influence on all the civilizations of the world. However, printed and written words can say something only to people who know the language the words belong to. Even then, they have meaning only for people who have learned to read.

This is where signs come in. It is hard for most people to learn many different languages, but it is easy to learn the meaning of signs and symbols. Take our Arabic numerals, for example: 1, 2, 3, and so on. These are signs. People who speak French or Spanish or Russian or any one of a number of other languages know these numerals and the signs we use in working with them. Many of these people also use our punctuation marks. The arrow is another sign that is known all over the world. People can understand its meaning even if they cannot read a word.

Information and ideas are communicated to us by the color, size, and shape of things. We recognize the letters on the page we are reading by their shape. That is how we recognize most of the signs we use. Shapes are easier to remember than colors.

Some of the simplest signs have played an important part in the history of the world. Think how difficult it would be to add or subtract, multiply or divide, without a zero. Yet when the zero was first invented, no one knew how important it was to become.

Imagine reading a book with no periods, commas, or question marks. It would not be impossible, but it would be difficult. How would you know when an idea ended? These signs, too, have probably achieved an importance far beyond what was expected when they were first used.

Other signs have had nothing whatever to do with the history of the world, but they are understood by thousands of people just the same. For example, take a few of the signs used in comic strips. A "balloon" around a group of words indicates that someone is speaking them. Footprints show that someone is going somewhere. Everyone knows that "sawing wood" means "snoring" or "sleeping." A drawing of a light bulb surrounded by rays of light tells us that an idea is lighting up in the mind of a comic-strip character. Stars are used to indicate a bump on the head—"seeing stars." And] % ! * ' / = # will do for anything that is considered unprintable.

In our modern world, more and more signs and symbols are being used all the time. Designers are at work inventing new signs for international use. Organizations and governments all over the world are asking for more signs that people everywhere can understand.

Why do we need so many new signs? We might do without them if everyone in the world spoke the same language. We might do without them if most people stayed in their own tight little corner of the world, without bothering about other people who speak languages different from their own. But that is not what the world is like today.

There are more people in the world than ever before. And more of them travel. Countries trade with other countries. People want to know how other people live in faraway places. They want to know about the arts in other countries, about science, sports, and many other things. Travelers need signs to help them find their way, especially to important services such as telephones, lunchrooms, rest rooms, hotels, and post offices. In short, signs and symbols help us to communicate with the whole world.

What exactly do we mean by signs and symbols? A sign is a mark, a design, or sometimes a picture that is commonly used to represent an idea or to convey certain information. Signs are often called symbols, and the two words are sometimes used interchangeably, even in this book. But, strictly speaking, a symbol is not the same as a sign.

Here is the simplest definition of "symbol": anything that stands for something else. For example, the bald eagle is a symbol of the United States. The owl is a symbol of wisdom. The lion is a symbol of courage. These are things you can see, but they represent qualities or ideas that you cannot see. A symbol often represents something invisible. Often, too, it represents something that has an important meaning for people.

All through history people have found that some ideas and feelings can be expressed better in symbols than in words. A symbol can help people to understand the unknown.

There are many kinds of signs and symbols. This book is about graphic signs and symbols—that is, those that can be written or drawn, printed or painted. Many of them are as old as the history of man. Others are completely new.

Here are a few samples of the signs and symbols you will meet in this book. How many do you recognize?

There is an old saying, "A single picture is worth a thousand words." The Chinese put it this way:

one hundred

hear(s)

are not

as good as

one

see.

Actually, this is not always true. There are ideas and information that can be explained only in words. But often a picture, or a sign or a symbol, really is worth a thousand words.

Some signs and symbols are simplified pictures of things. These are usually the easiest to understand. For example, this sign stands for forestry:

One tree stands for the many trees in the forest. This sign is not hard to understand, but you might not be sure of the meaning unless you were told. The meaning of most picture-signs must be learned. Their advantage is that they are easy to learn.

Ideas are harder to express in signs than things are. Graphic signs and symbols that represent ideas are often abstract—that is, their shape or design is not a picture of anything. The meaning of these must always be learned.

The plus sign + is an abstract sign. So are other mathematical signs, punctuation marks, and numerals. Some of them have different meanings in different uses, even for people who speak the same language. This sign − in a printed sentence is a dash, usually indicating an interruption in the meaning of the words. In mathematics, the same sign means "minus."

The arrow is a sign that is derived from a definite object, but it has become an abstract symbol used to express an idea. Two arrows can express still other ideas:

back and forth   *up and down*

Not everyone would agree with these interpretations, however. To some of the American Indians, arrows going back and forth meant war. To them, an arrow really meant an *arrow*.

Symbols can be hopelessly confusing when their meaning is not clear. There is a famous story that illustrates this:

More than 2,000 years ago, the Persian king Darius was trying to conquer a people called Scythians. He camped with his army on Scythian territory. Then he sent a message to the Scythian kings demanding that they send gifts of earth and water to him. These would symbolize surrender. All of Scythia, earth and water, would then be turned over to

Darius. Since he was a powerful king who had conquered many lands, Darius expected the Scythians to submit.

The Scythian kings did not send earth and water. They sent a messenger to Darius bearing different gifts—a bird, a mouse, a frog, and five arrows. (They might have sent a drawing of these things, but they chose instead to send the actual objects.) It was up to Darius and his advisers to figure out the meaning of the message.

Darius thought the message meant: The Scythians are surrendering themselves and their earth and water to us because the mouse is a creature of the earth, a frog is a creature of water, and a bird is most like a horse. And the arrows show that the Scythians are turning their weapons over to us. (It is not clear why Darius thought a bird was like a horse!)

One of Darius' advisers, Gobryas, had a different idea. This is his interpretation of the message, as told long ago by the Greek historian Herodotus: "Unless you become birds, Persians, and fly up into the sky, or mice and hide you in the earth, or frogs and leap into the lakes, you will be shot by these arrows and never return home."

Darius wanted to conquer the Scythians, but he wanted an easy victory. He hoped that his interpretation of the message was correct, but he was afraid that Gobryas was right. His army was tired from much fighting, and he knew that the Scythians were fresh and strong. After consulting his advisers, Darius ordered his army to go quietly away. The Scythians, who had no intention whatever of surrendering, pursued the Persians but never did catch up with them. Gobryas' interpretation of the message happened to be the right one.

From the point of view of communicating a message, the bird, the mouse, the frog, and five arrows were practically useless symbols. Figuring out their meaning was almost like a guessing game. But, of course, the Scythians had not intended their message to be easily understood.

To communicate any sort of information or ideas, signs and symbols must have an established meaning that is known to all the people who use them. In this book you can read about signs and symbols that have been used in the past, those that are important to us today, and some interesting possibilities for new signs in the future.

2/

Picture
Writing

In the days when people lived in caves, more than 50,000 years ago, no one knew how to write. There was no alphabet. There were no written signs.

If a cave man wanted to communicate with someone, he could talk. He had few words, some of them grunts and noises, but he could get an idea across. He could also gesture with his hands, his head, and even sometimes with his feet. But that was all. He had no way of conveying a message to someone who wasn't there. He could not leave a note for his wife when she was out picking berries and he was going to hunt in the far woods. He could not write down the story of his successful hunt for a saber-tooth tiger so that other people would know about it, in other years.

Man began to make pictures in very early times. The first ones were made for magic. A man would draw a picture of an animal on the walls of his cave. He was sure that making the picture would help him to catch the animal itself when he went out to hunt. This was an important kind of magic because the man needed the meat of animals to keep himself and his family alive.

These pictures were often made deep inside caves, where it was dark. It was not considered important for people to see them. This man was not trying to communicate with other people in his paintings.

Early man drew first with charcoal—that is, burnt sticks from his fire. Later, he learned to use wild plants to make colors for his painting, and to make brushes from wood or bone. And he painted not only inside caves but often on the walls of cliffs. Sometimes he carved pictures on the face of the rock with a sharp stone or pieces of ivory.

The earliest pictures showed animals standing still, but before long man started to put action into his paintings and carvings. He showed animals running away from the hunter, animals fighting with one another, animals eating grass in the fields.

Sometimes he drew cave men at a feast after a good day's hunting. In short, he was now telling stories in pictures. And he was making records of important events. Other people could look at his paintings and see what had happened. They could feel a little of what he had felt. Years later, he himself could go back to a painting and enjoy his own record of a great hunt or a great feast.

Still, these pictures were not the same as writing, and they were not signs for communication. An early artist could paint or carve an animal or a man any way he wished. Other people might recognize what his picture represented—if it looked enough like the subject. However, they could understand what was going on in the picture only if it was something they were already familiar with. A stranger who had always lived alone with just his family might not have any idea what a picture of a tribal feast was all about.

We call pictures that are used to tell stories "pictographs." "Picto" means "picture." "Graph" is from an ancient Greek word that means "writing." Probably "writing" originally meant "to cut." Many early pictographs were cut in stone or on pieces of bone.

cave painting

Picture writing has limitations. As we have seen, a picture usually has meaning only for someone who already knows something about the subject. You can make your own example to illustrate this point. Suppose you wanted to draw the story of a picnic in the woods. You begin with two people walking along, one of them carrying a basket. (You might draw extra lines alongside, to represent more people.)

Then you draw a picture of two people sitting under some trees taking sandwiches from the basket. (Or are they putting them *into* the basket?) You make the pictures with as few lines as possible, in order to finish quickly. Perhaps your pictures look like this:

To someone else, the first picture might look like two people on their way to a supermarket. The second one might suggest, to still another person, an excursion to pick berries.

Pictographs can be used as writing only when their meaning is known to a number of people. This is true whether the meaning of a pictograph is easy to guess or whether it must be learned.

Pictographs have other limitations. There are a great many things you cannot make a picture of at all. How would you draw the wind? You might make a picture of tree branches bending in the wind, but you could not be sure that anyone else would know what you meant. A person looking at your picture might think you meant a bent tree, or just a lot of leaves.

How would you make a picture of happiness? Would you draw a smiling face? For unhappiness, a pair of eyes with tears falling down? You could still not be sure of getting your meaning across.

In spite of these drawbacks, for a long time people kept on with picture writing. They had no better way of recording the things that were important to them. Some of the same pictures were made over and over again because the same things were important to many people.

It took quite a long time to make a good picture. So, as the same picture was drawn again and again, by different people, parts of it gradually began to be left out, to make it easier to draw. Finally, after many years, a greatly simplified drawing or design came to stand for the whole thing. People who were familiar with the things represented could learn what these pictographs meant. Then the pictographs could be useful.

The American Indians had a very expressive picture writing. They sent messages and recorded important events on birch bark and on the skins of animals. Paintings and carvings on the face of rocks also preserved the story of Indian life in some sections of North America.

The Indians used many colors in their painting—reds, greens, yellows, blues. The colors were made from earth, flowers, and various plants that the Indians dried, crushed to form a powder, and mixed with water.

Another form of Indian picture writing was done with wampum, the shell beads the Indians used for trading. Pictographs were woven into wampum belts to record important events such as peace treaties between the tribes. The belts were considered to be valuable records. The most famous treaty belt is the one Indian chiefs presented to William Penn, founder of Pennsylvania, on the shore of the Delaware River in 1682. This belt shows an Indian and a white man holding hands in a gesture of peace and friendship that was never forgotten by either Penn or the Indians.

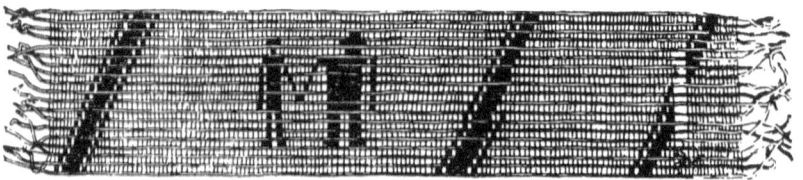

All Indian tribes did not use the same signs to represent the same things. For example, there are several Indian pictographs for "sun":

"To cry" in one Indian sign is this:

Another Indian sign for crying shows just an eye with tears falling down.

This means "water":

Here is an Indian sign for "sky":

A blackened sky means "night":

The time of day is conveniently indicated by a line projecting from the sign for "sky" to show the position of the sun:

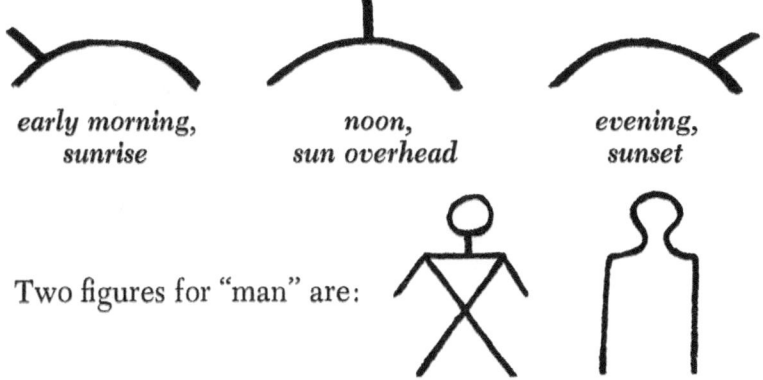

| *early morning, sunrise* | *noon, sun overhead* | *evening, sunset* |

Two figures for "man" are:

A wise man, on the other hand, has a sort of glow about him:

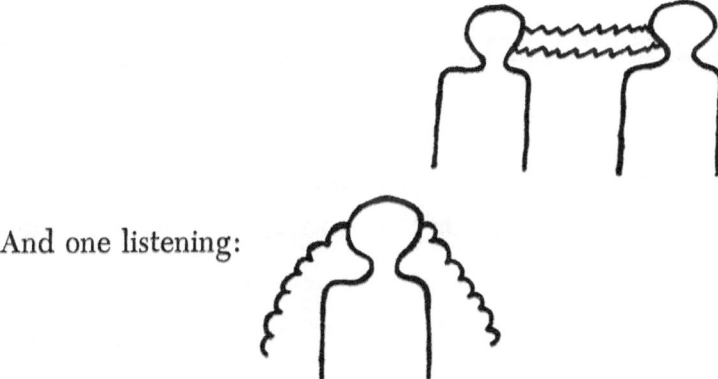

His wisdom was thought to come from the spirit above.

Here are two people talking together:

And one listening:

More than one man could be shown by drawing the required number of figures. This was slow. It was easier to show how many there were by drawing little lines underneath the picture or beside it:

three men   five women

Long lines drawn underneath the figures had a different meaning:

brothers   sisters

Little lines drawn beside a sign meaning "day" might tell the number of days. Or these lines might have a slightly different meaning:

third day   sixth day

This form was used in dating letters.

Most of these pictographs are from the Plains Indians, but other Indians also did picture writing.

Not all the old Indian inscriptions that have been found can be read by people today, but the "winter counts" of the Dakota Indians are relatively easy to read. A winter count was a kind of history. The most important event of each year was recorded in a single sign painted on a buffalo robe or on a special tent. The most famous of these winter counts was kept by the Dakota Indians for seventy-one years.

Many Indian signs had to do with war or peace. This was one symbol for "peace":

You cannot fight with a broken arrow.

Here is a brief, made-up story told in Indian picture writing. As you will see, not all the words can be put directly into pictures. And there is nothing in the pictures to tell whether the action took place in the past or whether it is taking place right now.

Left to right:

Translated into English, the story reads: One morning when it was raining, four hungry men left their tepee and went to the river. By noon they had caught many fish. The sun came out. The four men returned to their tepee in the evening.

There is a famous petition in pictures that Chippewa Indian chiefs sent to the United States Government in 1849. These Indians lived in Wisconsin, near Lake Superior. They wanted the Government to allow them to settle near some small lakes where they could harvest wild rice. There they proposed to live peaceably.

In the first picture, shown opposite, the chiefs are represented by the animals or birds that were their own chosen symbols. The leading chief is represented by a crane. Lines extend from the eyes of all the other animals to the eye of the crane. This means that all the chiefs see "eye to eye." They agree on the petition.

The heart of each animal is also connected by a line with the heart of the crane. These lines show that all the chiefs *feel* the same way about the petition and have the same purpose in sending it.

Long parallel lines indicate Lake Superior. A path leads from the lake to the four small "rice lakes" where the Indians propose to settle. From the eye of the crane a line extends forward, toward Washington, D. C., the destination of the petition.

How could more be said in a single picture?

The Leni-Lenape Indians, also called the Delawares, produced a remarkable song in picture writing. The pictures, painted on separate sticks, told about the creation of the universe. The Indians knew the meaning of each picture. Here are some of them, with a free translation of their meaning as

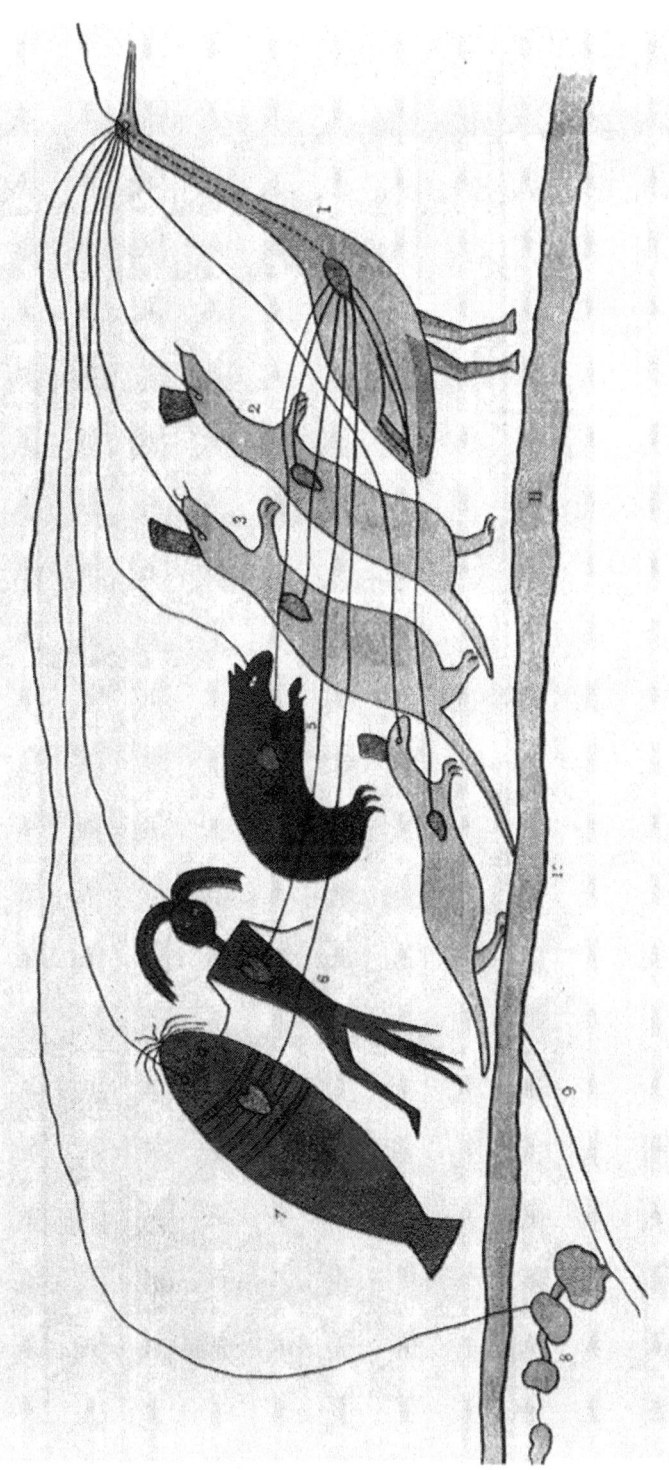

First picture of Chippewa Indian Chiefs' petition.

given by the Indians themselves. The Indians' god is called Manito.

At first, forever, lost in space, everywhere, the great Manito was.

He made the land and the sky.

He made the sun, the moon, and the stars.

Then the wind blew hard, and it cleared, and the water flowed off far and strong.

And groups of islands grew and remained.

The great Manito spoke to the beings, mortals, souls and all.

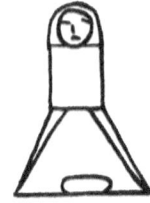

And ever after he was a Manito to men, and their grandfather.

He gave the first mother, the mother of beings.

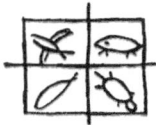 He gave the fish, he gave the turtles, he gave the beasts, he gave the birds.

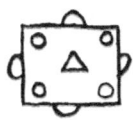 All beings were then friendly.

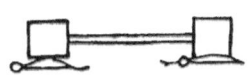 And all this took place of old on the earth, beyond the great tidewater.

The American Indians used many of their pictographs on pottery, in beadwork, and in weaving blankets. Sometimes the pictographs were used just for decoration. Sometimes they conveyed a message. At other times, they were for magic, to help bring good luck or prosperity.

Indian figures drawn or painted on rocks are called "petrographs," meaning "written on stone." Those that were carved on rocks are called "petroglyphs."

Indian picture writing is no longer widely used, but it served a very real purpose in the past.

The Eskimos in the far north have their own picture writing even today. When times are hard, an Eskimo can leave a message scratched on a piece of wood where someone will find it and send help. The following message was actually used:

(1)　　　(2)　　　(3)　　　(4)

Here is the explanation of the figures:

(1) A line represents a canoe. This shows that the people in trouble are fishermen.

(2) A man with his arms spread means "nothing."

(3) A figure with hand to mouth indicates "eating." This figure also points toward the figure for "house" (4).

The message reads: Nothing to eat in the house. Starving. Help!

South of the United States, in Mexico, the ancient Aztecs developed a complicated and colorful civilization. Their writing, like that of the American Indians, was done with pictures. These had a distinctive style of their own. Unfortunately, very few examples of this writing remain because the Spanish explorers destroyed all of them that they could find.

The following are day signs from an Aztec Calendar Stone. Each day of the Aztec twenty-day month had its own picture-sign.

house   **deer**   **water**   **flower**

In parts of what is now southern Mexico and Central America, the ancient Mayas carved their extremely complex picture writing on stone and wrote in books made of barkcloth paper. Most of these books were burned by the Spanish conquerors. Very little is known about the meaning of the Mayan writing that remains. Here is part of a Mayan inscription:

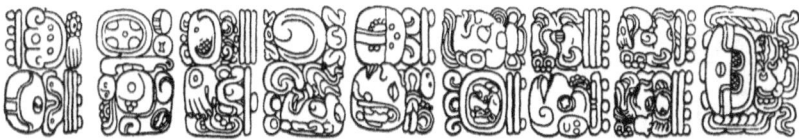

The picture writings described in this chapter never developed into signs that represented the *sound* of spoken words or of parts of words. Other people did develop such signs, however, and that is how alphabets came into being.

3/

From
Picture
Writing to
Alphabets

Thousands of years ago, in ancient times, some very ingenious people lived in Egypt, along the River Nile in north-
eastern Africa. They developed a system of writing called
"hieroglyphics," a word that comes from two ancient Greek
words meaning "sacred carvings."

Hieroglyphic writing included many signs that can be
called pictographs. They are simplified pictures of things,
some of them quite recognizable. But hieroglyphic writing
was not picture writing in the same sense as American Indian
picture writing. It was more than that, and it was much
more complex.

It is hard even for experts to know exactly what happened
so long ago. It seems likely that Egyptian hieroglyphic writing began as real picture writing. Let's look at some of the
signs:

sun   *mountain*   *fish*   *star*

The fish is a quite recognizable fish. The star looks something like a star. The sun and the mountain might be hard to figure out. Once known, however, they would be easy to remember.

It is hard to make pictures of such things as the sky and water. This is how the Egyptians did it:

sky (a cover)   *water*

(Notice how similar the sign for "water" is to the American Indian pictograph for "water.")

Written signs like the two above represent not just the things themselves, but also the idea behind the things. When the sky is shown as a cover, the sign represents someone's feeling about the sky. The sky was thought to be a cover over all the world, resting on the mountains on either edge of it.

The hieroglyph for "water" represents its motion. (How else could you make a simple picture of water?)

Egyptian signs were also combined to produce new meanings. A closed flower under the cover of the sky meant "darkness":

The same sign with the addition of the sun low in the sky meant "evening":

The sky with a star or a lamp meant "night":

"Rain" was represented by water running down from the cover of the sky:

Action is still harder to represent in written signs. The Egyptians did it by drawing something that you would naturally think of in connection with the action. Two legs meant "to go":

Two eyes meant "to see." Eyes with drops of water coming from them meant "to weep":

Signs made to represent the idea behind a thing are called "ideographs"—that is, "idea writings." Sometimes the same ideographs developed among people in widely separated parts of the world. An eye with a tear coming from it meant "to weep" in the written language of prehistoric people in Central America. The Chinese in ancient times had the same ideograph.

Sometimes the same hieroglyph, unchanged, could be both a pictograph and an ideograph. We have seen that ⊙ meant "sun." It also meant "day." The first of these is something that you can see and make a picture of. The second represents something you cannot see. That is why it is an ideograph.

When the sun was pictured sending forth rays, the ideograph meant "splendid light," or "glory." Perhaps this was what the inventor of the sign thought of as he watched the bright rays of the sun.

The hieroglyph for "star" sometimes stood for just the star of dawn. It also meant "to pray." Egyptians often prayed at dawn, when only a few last stars could be seen.

The plural for "star," any number more than one, was a picture of three stars:

Other plurals were made in the same way.

Pictographs and ideographs were only part of hieroglyphic writing. Long ago, at the beginning of Egypt's recorded history, there were hieroglyphic signs that represented, not things or ideas, but parts of spoken words—that is, syllables. There were also about twenty-four signs that stood for single spoken sounds. These might be called letter-signs.

Egyptian letter-signs worked like this:

Here is the sign for "mouth":

This was originally a pictograph, and the Egyptians kept on using it that way as well as for a letter-sign. The Egyptian word for "mouth" (in our spelling) was *ro*. The sign for "mouth" was used to stand for the sound of *r*. That is, the sign for the whole word was used to represent just the sound at the beginning of the word.

The sound of *n* was written:

This was the wavy line for "water," which in Egyptian was *nu*. Again, the sign for the whole word was used to represent the sound at its beginning.

Egyptian sound-pictures looked like pictographs, and in fact many of them were adapted from pictographs. However, their use to represent sounds was quite different from the use of pictographs to represent things.

Pictures of things, and idea-pictures, and sound-signs were all used together in Egyptian writing. This was complicated. And some hieroglyphs had several meanings. Combinations of signs were often used to represent a single thing or idea, but the signs in these combinations were not always the same.

For example, here are two ways of writing the same word. One is a combination of signs. The other is a single sign. Both mean "writing." They occur within a few words of each other on an Egyptian document.

The first two signs at the left spell out the sound of the Egyptian word for "writing," *schai*. Then, in case this is not clear, a figure of a man in the act of writing is added.

The single sign for "writing" at the right does not spell out the sound of the word at all. Instead, it is a picture of writing materials: a split reed on the left, attached to a cord which has a scribe's ink bottle hanging from it.

The following combination meant "thirst":

The first two signs are letter-signs representing *ab*, the Egyptian word for "thirst." To be sure this was clear, however, the sign for "water" was added, and following that, a man pointing to his mouth.

Pictographs and ideographs were often added to other signs in this way, to help explain their meaning. This practice made the whole process of writing much more complicated. Hieroglyphic writing was too unwieldy for everyday use, but the Egyptians kept on using it on the walls of temples and in the tombs of their kings. For more practical purposes, a sort of shorthand known as "hieratic writing" was developed. It was done with a reed pen on the Egyptian paperlike material called papyrus. Hieratic writing was a simplified form of hieroglyphic writing. There were just as many signs, but they were drawn with fewer strokes. Later, still simpler writing called "demotic writing" came into use.

Egyptian hieroglyphs had beauty and style. Fascinating figures of animals and people, snakes and birds and bees, signs representing the sun, the sky, and the moon, and many others followed one after another. But this was a cumbersome way of writing, even in the hieratic and demotic forms.

The ancient Egyptians could have given up their elaborate system of pictographs and ideographs entirely. In its place, they could have developed an alphabet as practical as our own. As we have seen, Egyptian writing included about twenty-four signs that stood for single spoken sounds. Every word in the Egyptian language could have been written with these signs.

If the Egyptians had used their sound signs as an alphabet, many more people could have learned to read and write. But the scribes who did the writing in those days did not want more people to know how to write. They had spent many years learning the very special art of writing, and they had great influence on the rulers of the country. Writing was used primarily to glorify the gods the people worshiped, and the kings who ruled them. It was called "the speech of the gods."

Writing was a sacred mystery to most of the people. The scribes wanted it to remain a mystery because their power depended on it. Hieroglyphic writing could be very useful—but only to those who knew its meaning.

No one uses hieroglyphic writing today, or hieratic, or demotic. Egyptians now speak and write an entirely different language, Arabic, which they acquired along with the Mohammedan religion.

Northeast of Egypt was the land known as Mesopotamia, between the Tigris and Euphrates rivers. There, in very early times, lived the Sumerians. These people used pictographs to record their ideas and their business transactions, just as the Egyptians did. Like all pictographs, those of the Sumerians started out as drawings of definite things, and then were simplified. Different people draw and simplify in different ways. The Sumerian pictographs were not at all like the Egyptian ones.

Sumerian pictographs eventually changed to very stylized signs quite different from the original ones. The sign for "bird," for instance, changed like this:

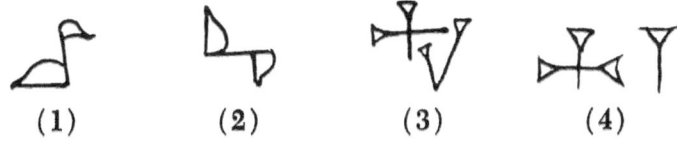

The wedge-shaped marks were made in wet clay with a stylus, a sharp-tipped reed. This writing is called "cuneiform," from a Latin word meaning "wedge-shaped."

Cuneiform writing was used throughout western Asia long after the Sumerian nation had ceased to exist. In time, some of the signs were used to represent the sounds of words or parts of words. But there was still no workable alphabet.

Until recently, the Chinese people had no alphabet. Their written language is made up of characters that developed from early pictographs and ideographs. Over thousands of years, these characters changed from simple pictorial forms to elaborate patterns made with the strokes of a brush.

Most of the Chinese characters used today are ideographs, but some can still be called pictographs. The character for "tree," for example, still looks something like a tree: 木

Other characters are more complicated. Some are pictographs combined to make ideographs. Here is one:

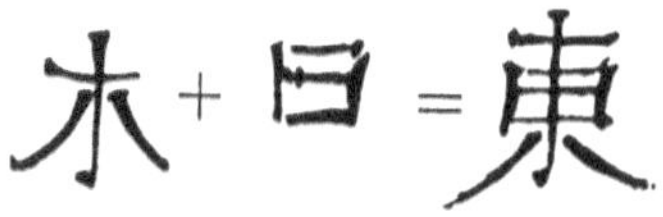

木 + 日 = 東

tree + sun = east

The east is where the sun can be seen shining through the trees.

The character for "happy" is a combination of the signs for "wife" and "child":

女子

The following chart shows how a few modern Chinese characters developed from early pictographs:

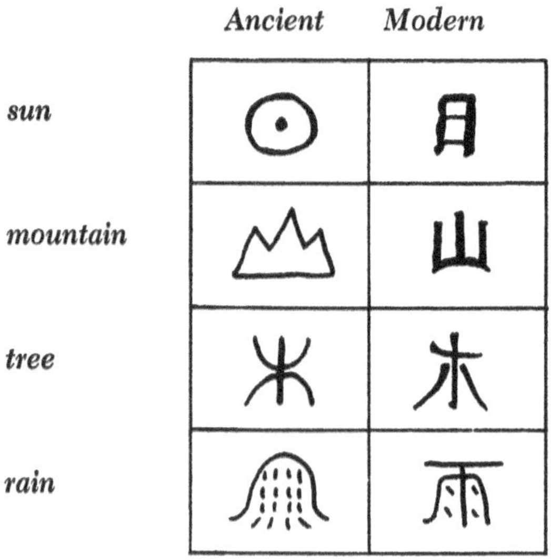

	Ancient	Modern
sun	⊙	日
mountain	⋀⋀	山
tree	米	木
rain	⋀	雨

The Chinese can express very complex ideas with their characters, and anyone who has learned the meaning of the characters can read Chinese even if he cannot speak it. This is especially useful for the Chinese because their spoken language has many different versions, or dialects.

It takes some 40,000 signs to cover everything in the Chinese written language, though an educated person can get along nicely with 6,000 to 8,000. This is a difficult language for anyone to learn to read, even for the Chinese. In earlier days, relatively few Chinese did know how to read. Most of them simply did not have the time or opportunity to learn.

Recently, the Chinese government has been trying to do something about the problem. Hundreds of the most common Chinese characters have been simplified so that they are easier to write. A written alphabet, similar to our own, has also been adopted. Although it does not entirely take the place of the traditional characters, it makes the written language easier to learn by providing sound-signs to be used along with the characters. Without this improvement, most of the people in China would still not know how to read.

On the next page is a sample of present-day Chinese writing, taken from a letter written by a little girl in the British Crown Colony of Hong Kong.

Compare it with the Japanese advertisement on page 49. Japanese writing is derived from Chinese characters and is also very complicated, though there is a simpler set of signs for telegrams and advertisements.

Quite different pictographs, in different languages, can be

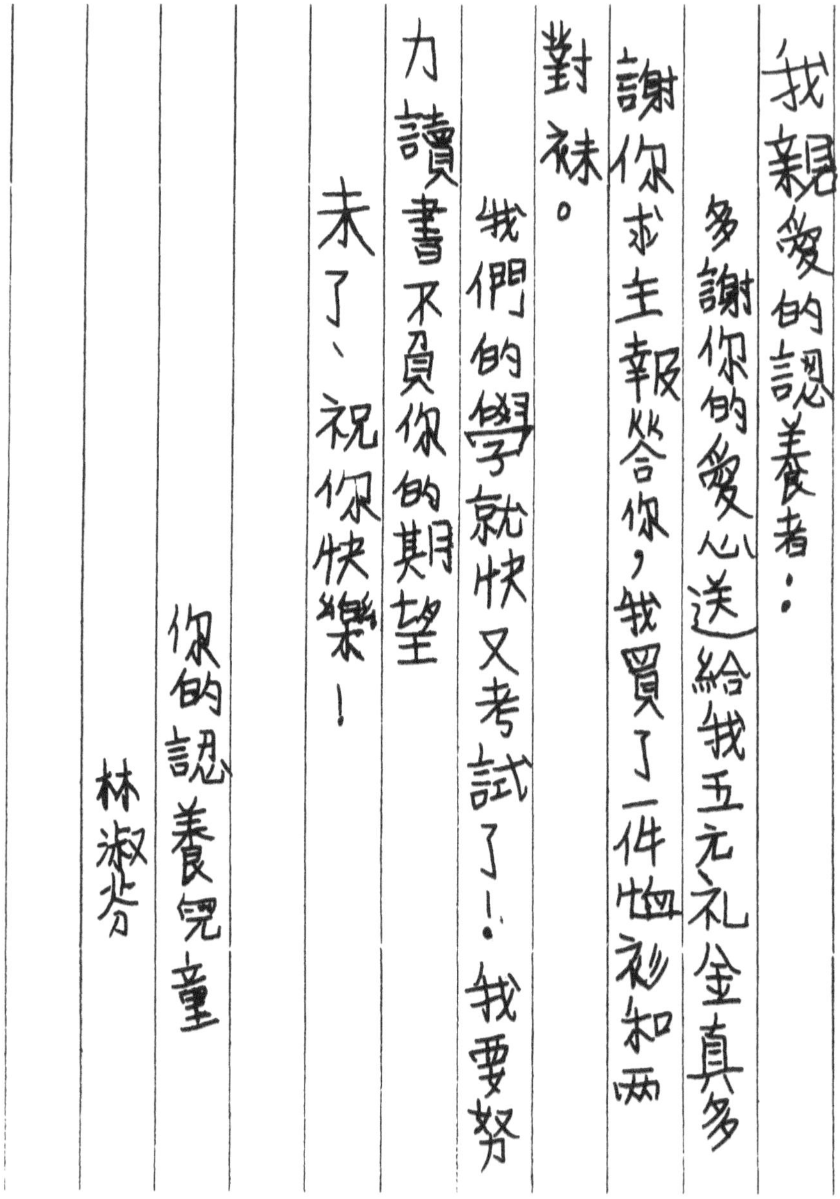

我親愛的認養者：

多謝你的愛心送給我五元礼金真多

謝你求主報答你，我買了一件恤衫和兩

對袜。

我們的學就快又考試了！我要努

力讀書不負你的期望

末了、祝你快樂！

你的認養兒童

林淑芬

Chinese handwriting

Japanese advertisement

used to represent the same things. We can see this by comparing, on a chart, a few pictographs that were used in ancient times by the Sumerians, the Egyptians, the Chinese, and, more recently, by the American Indians.

The Chinese character for "sky" on our chart looks like a man. There was a reason for this. The sky is the highest part of the universe. The head is the highest part of the human body. So the sign for "sky" (and also "heaven") shows a man's head at the top of his body.

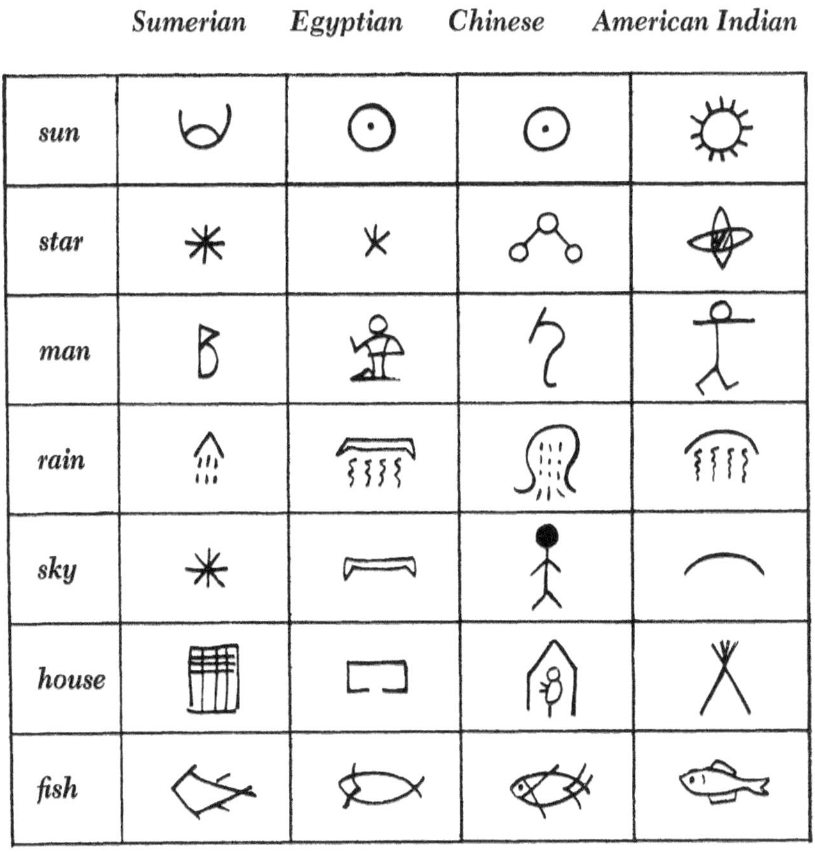

	Sumerian	Egyptian	Chinese	American Indian
sun				
star				
man				
rain				
sky				
house				
fish				

Sometimes one language actually had more than one pictograph representing the same thing, though only one appears on the chart. And there were different pictographs at different periods.

An alphabet is essentially a series of letters (or signs) used in writing a language. The earliest workable alphabet we know much about is that of the ancient Semites. The Semites lived on the Sinai Peninsula, on the shores of the Mediterranean Sea. Some of them worked for Egyptians. They had to keep records of their work, and they found the Egyptian writing too complicated. So they took the Egyptian signs that represented single sounds, adapted them to their own language, and thus developed an alphabet of sound-symbols.

The Phoenicians, who lived in the same part of the world as the Semites, also needed to keep records. They sailed the Mediterranean, trading with other countries, and they had to have an efficient way of keeping track of the things they bought and sold. The Phoenicians saw the advantages of the Semitic system and adapted it to their own writing. They had twenty-two letter-pictures in their alphabet, almost 3,000 years ago.

The Greeks, who were also traders on the Mediterranean Sea, borrowed the Phoenician letters, changed them, and added to them. One thing they added was vowels, which made written words much easier to read. With the Greeks, writing at last became a tool for recording even the most complicated ideas.

The Romans, still farther west on the Mediterranean, took over the Greek alphabet and changed it even more. Many of the letters that had angles in the Greek alphabet acquired curves in the Roman. This is the alphabet we use today, 2,000 years later.

The letters of our alphabet are not pictographs or ideographs because they do not, by themselves, represent things or ideas. They represent the sounds that make up our spoken words. Nevertheless, it may be interesting to see how some of our letters probably developed from earlier pictographs.

Egyptian	*Semitic*	*Phoenician*	*Greek*	*Roman*
ox				A
house				B
door				D
snake				N

Let's see if we can clarify some of the differences between pictographs and ideographs, and the letters of an alphabet. Pictographs and most ideographs do not depend on a particular language. People may have to be told their meaning in the first place, but then they can understand them, no matter what language they speak.

It is different with signs made to represent sounds, as our letters do. You have to know the spoken language that is being represented. If you don't, the written signs mean nothing. If your language is English, for example, you can read English words written with the letters of our alphabet, as you are doing now. If you speak only French, you can read French words written with the same alphabet, but not English words. (Only a few words belong to both languages.)

But now look at this line printed in Burmese, a language of Southeast Asia:

ကမ္ဘာသားတွေသုံးဘို့ ရေ

Burmese is written in an alphabet entirely different from ours. To read Burmese, you would have to learn a new alphabet as well as new words.

The sounds of whole words, or parts of words, can be represented by pictures, as they are in a rebus. A rebus is a way of expressing words by pictures of things whose names sound like those words. Like this:

I   *can*   *knot (not)*   *fly*

This is not the same as using pictographs to represent the meaning of words. It is a beginning of sound-signs. To understand a rebus, you must know the language it is written in.

The use of the letters of an alphabet to represent single spoken sounds is the most efficient way ever invented for writing down words. Letters that stand for sounds can be used over and over again in different combinations. All our words can be written with just the twenty-six letters of our alphabet. Compare this with the thousands of Egyptian hieroglyphs of ancient times and the thousands of Chinese characters still in use today.

The development of alphabets opened up enormous possibilities for communication. Many people still could not read or write, but those who learned how could send written messages to one another. They could keep a record of the events of the day. They could read what other people wrote.

There are about fifty alphabets in use today. Some are used for only one language, some for several. Our own alphabet is the most widely used. All the alphabets in the Western World can be traced back to the Semitic alphabet invented 3,000 years ago, and beyond that, to the Egyptians, who were using alphabetic signs more than 2,000 years before anyone else had thought of them.

Efficient as they are, alphabets can never entirely take the place of signs and symbols. Some ideas are better expressed by symbols, even today. There is still a need for communication across the languages of the world.

4/

Numerals
and
Other Signs

The signs that we use to represent numbers are known to people in most parts of the world, whatever their language. We call these signs "numerals," and there are ten of them: 1, 2, 3, 4, 5, 6, 7, 8, 9, and 0. With various combinations of these numerals, any conceivable number can be written.

Numbers had names in spoken languages before there were any written numerals. Each language today has its own names for numbers, and they differ greatly. For example, in English we say "five." The French say *cinq*, the Swedish *fem*, the Spanish *cinco*. But people who speak any of these languages can all read the numeral 5.

Our numerals are especially useful to people who do business all over the world. It is hard enough to carry on business transactions when the language is not the same. It would be almost impossible for businessmen to buy and sell goods if they could not read each other's written numbers.

Numeral systems different from ours do exist, however, and millions of people use them. Chinese and Japanese numerals are entirely different from ours. People who speak Arabic have still another set of numerals. These people are mostly followers of the Mohammedan religion, in the Middle East and parts of Asia and Africa.

In the earliest times numbers were, of course, not written down at all. At first, it was seldom necessary even to count. But, in time, counting became important. People wanted to know how many sheep and cattle they had in their herds. Hunters liked to keep track of the numbers of animals they had killed. Men counted their tools and weapons.

Counting could be done by collecting sticks or pebbles, one for each thing being counted. Or notches could be cut in a piece of wood. Often, it was most convenient just to count up to ten on one's fingers. Sticks or pebbles might be lost, but not fingers.

Eventually, as people began to use numbers more and more, they gave them names. The first written numbers were used by wise men to keep track of the days of the year. These men made the first calendars.

The Egyptians had written numerals at least 5,000 years ago. The shapes they used were not always identical; but the system went about like this (there was no zero):

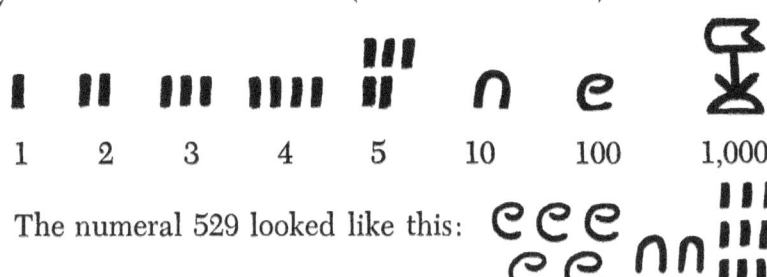

The numeral 529 looked like this:

It was extremely difficult to do any kind of figuring with these numerals. Figuring was left to wise men and scribes. To most of the people, working with numerals seemed like magic. Those who had the ability to work with numerals were thought to have power over the lives of others.

In Mesopotamia, the land between the Tigris and Euphrates rivers, the Sumerians developed numerals at about the same time the Egyptians did. The Sumerian numbers were made with the same wedge-shaped tool used to make Sumerian letters. Thus:

The Sumerians also had no zero, and figuring with these numerals was just as complicated as with the Egyptian.

The Chinese had a system of numerals at a very early time, too. At first, they would put small counting sticks on a table in appropriate patterns, like this:

I	II	III	IIII	IIIII	T	TT	TTT	TTTT	—
1	2	3	4	5	6	7	8	9	10

=	☰	⊥	⊥	|
20	50	60	70	100 (stick placed at left)

Modern Chinese numerals developed from these patterns. The first three have changed very little. The others have changed a great deal.

一	二	三	四	五	十	十二
1	2	3	4	5	10	13 (10 plus 3)

Notice that the shape of the strokes in numerals 1, 2, 3 has changed. These are no longer sticks. They are ink strokes made with a fine brush.

The Egyptian and Sumerian numerals were not adopted by any other people of ancient times. The Phoenician traders, once they had developed their alphabet, used its letters for writing numbers. The first letter, *aleph*, represented the number "one." *Beth*, the second letter, was "two," and so on.

The Greeks followed the same system. But the Romans invented a system of their own, using letters in a different way.

I	II	III	IIII or IV	V	VI	VII	VIII
1	2	3	4	5	6	7	8

IX	X	L	C	D	M
9	10	50	100	500	1,000

For some of the larger numbers, the Romans used the first letter of the number word. C stood for *centum*, meaning 100. M was for *mille*, meaning 1,000.

Roman numerals were used in Europe for centuries. Even after our present numerals were adopted for most purposes, Roman numerals were still used for keeping business accounts. Today, you can see them on some clock faces or sometimes on the chapter headings in books.

Roman numerals were neat and clear, but, like the Egyptian and Sumerian numerals, they were extremely clumsy to work with. For example, our number 3,656 would be

M M M D C L V I

Try multiplying this by VI!

Fortunately, most people in Roman times needed to do only the simplest arithmetic. Harder problems were solved by slaves, using an abacus, a device with movable counters on a series of rods. You may have seen a Chinese abacus. They are still used today.

In our own part of the world, the early Mayas in Central America used only three signs for writing numbers: a dot, a line, and an oval. With these they could write any number. Like this:

•	••	•••	••••	—	≐	⁜	⁖	⁘⁙	═
1	2	3	4	5	6	7	8	9	10

20 ⬭   100 ⬭

Mayan numerals were also clumsy to work with, but it was possible to figure with them.

The Mayas had another counting system that consisted of complicated drawings of different kinds of heads. Each head stood for a number or a combination of numbers. This system was even less practical than the dots, lines, and ovals.

Where, then, did our own practical numbers come from? We call them Arabic, but they are not Arabic at all. People who speak Arabic today use numerals quite different from ours. Our numerals came from the Hindus of India.

Like other people, the Hindus invented their own way of

writing. Their earliest numerals were similar to those of other people—just lines, representing counting sticks.

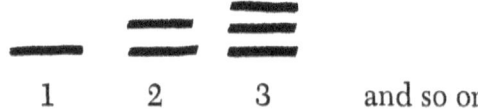

| 1 | 2 | 3 | and so on |

(We are not sure how all the earliest numbers were written.)

Now, if you write the Hindu "two" quite fast, the lines are likely to be joined together, like this:

And the "three," like this: Already it is possible to see our own 2 and 3 in these figures.

Of course, the figures changed as they were written over and over again. About 2,000 years ago, Hindu numbers looked like this:

१	२	३	४	५	६	७	८	९
1	2	3	4	5	6	7	8	9

With these nine numerals any number could be written. 2369 would be:

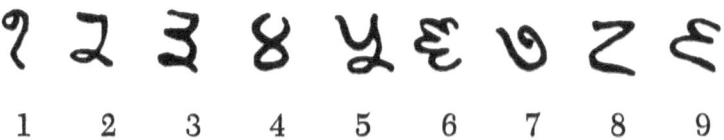

In figuring, it was important to put each numeral in the right position. For example, the Hindus at first wrote 501 by leaving an empty space between the 5 and the 1. This was sometimes confusing. You couldn't always be sure there was meant to be a space. So they invented the zero to put in the space. None of the other number systems had a zero. None of them were as practical as the Hindu. You can understand the importance of zero if you will try to do some figuring without it. Try multiplying 605 by 50—but without the zeros! (Leave a space instead.)

The ancient Hindus were traders. Their numerals were carried to the Arabs, who then took them to Europe. That is why we call our numerals Arabic, even though, in the form we know, they were never used by the Arabs.

The Arabic-Hindu numerals changed with use until they took on the forms we use today. Both our letters and our numerals have changed very little since the invention of the printing press.

Besides numerals, there are other signs that are used in connection with numbers—plus (+), for example, meaning "add." We are not sure where this came from. It may have started as a quick way of writing "and." Or it may come from the Italian abbreviation for the word meaning "plus," progressing like this:

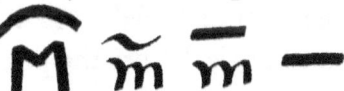

The minus sign (—) came from the Italian and Latin word *minus,* meaning "less." It was used for marking packages that were short in weight. The sign may have changed like this:

Like numerals, these signs are understood in most parts of the world.

Our dollar sign ($) belongs only to countries where money is measured in dollars. There are about a dozen such countries, but the sign is also understood by people in many other places.

The dollar sign looks like a combination of U. and S., the abbreviation for United States, but it is not. It came from the Spanish. Spain had a coin called a "Spanish dollar," though its official name was *peso de plata,* meaning "piece of silver." Other countries also had dollars. When the United States Government first started minting money, it decided to call the principal unit a "dollar." This was made the same size and weight as the Spanish *peso de plata.*

The sign that was chosen to represent the United States dollar was already in use by the Spanish. In its earliest form, the sign had been an 8 and a P written together. The P stood for "peso" and the 8 was for eight "reals." Eight Spanish reals equaled a dollar in value. Then the P was omitted and slanting lines were added. Our dollar sign grew from its original form in this fashion:

There is a handy sign for "and" that is used in a number of languages: &. It used to be written simply *et,* which meant "and" in Latin, the language of the ancient Romans. *Et* still means "and" in Italian, French, and other West European languages. It changed as it was written by the scribes who produced books before the printing press was invented. Like this:

When the doctor writes a prescription for medicine, he uses a slip of paper that has the following sign printed in the upper left corner: ℞

This sign was used in Italy to represent the word *recipe*, meaning "take," but the sign itself dates back to ancient times. Roman physicians then used the sign of the planet Jupiter to invoke the aid of Jupiter himself, father of the Roman gods.

In the Middle Ages, the sign changed until it took the form that doctors use today.

Punctuation marks are among the most useful signs in the world. They have much the same form in many written and printed languages. The earliest manuscripts written by scribes usually had no punctuation marks at all. This must have made them hard to read, but since very few people learned to read anyway, no one was concerned about making reading easier.

The ancient Greeks remedied the situation. They invented such marks as the comma, colon, semicolon, and period. These were first used in printed books almost 2,000 years later, by an Italian printer named Aldus Manutius, who was a great admirer of the Greeks. Most of the punctuation marks he used were like the Greek, but some were changed. The ancient Greek question mark was like our semicolon. Here is the way it changed:

﹔	﹖	?	¿!
Greek	*Latin*	*English*	*Spanish*

(Spanish has one mark at the beginning of a question, the other at the end.) Manutius gave the original Greek question mark its present name and use. We call this mark a semicolon.

It was hundreds of years before punctuation marks were used in the same way by all writers and printers. Now there is general agreement about their form and use. They make reading much easier, in any language.

Music is printed and written with its own system of signs. To read music, you must know the meaning of these signs. The notes used in written music are abstract signs, each one representing a tone, a musical sound, to be made by a human voice or a musical instrument. Originally, these signs were only dots and accent marks that were written above the words of a song, as a guide for singers. Later, when they were made with a wide-nibbed pen, they changed like this:

The oval shape of the notes we see today developed when the notes were drawn with a fine pen.

Dots and accent marks written above the words of a song were not of very great help to singers until someone thought of adding first one, then several, horizontal lines to show exactly how high or low the sounds were supposed to be. In time, five evenly spaced, horizontal lines came into use. This is the staff used in written music today.

Notes are written on the lines of the staff and in the spaces between the lines. The location of a note on the staff shows the pitch of the tone it represents—that is, how high or low the sound is. The length of time a note is to be held is shown by its design. The whole note is held the longest, the half note only half as long. Then there is a quarter note, an eighth note, and so on.

whole note   *half note*   *quarter note*   *eighth note*

The notes are named for the first seven letters of the alphabet: A, B, C, D, E, F, G. The same notes occur at higher and lower pitches, and so the seven letters are repeated over and over again.

On the staff, at the beginning of each line of written music, there is a sign called a "clef." The clef tells us the names and the pitch of the notes that are written on the lines of the staff and in the spaces. There are several clefs in music. This one is the G or treble clef:

This clef tells us that a note placed on the second line from the bottom of the staff is G.

In fact, the G clef was originally a simple letter G drawn around the second line from the bottom. It changed in time to the elaborate design that is used today, but the widest part of the clef sign still curls around the line for G.

Since there are a number of G's, at different pitches, we need to know which one is indicated by the G clef. It is always the first G above Middle C. Middle C is the C nearest the middle of the piano keyboard. Once the position of G is known, we can tell the names and pitch of other notes on the staff.

Middle C D E F G A B C D E F G
(Notice the extra line drawn in for Middle C.)

When the F or bass clef appears on the staff at the beginning of a line of music, we know that a note placed on the second line from the *top* is the first F *below* Middle C. From this, we can tell the names and pitch of other notes written on the staff.

G A B C D E F G A B C
(Notice again the extra line drawn in for Middle C.)

This clef was originally a letter F. A pair of dots now takes the place of the bar of the F.

There are many other signs in written music. All of them have a long history, and all have definite meaning for the musician. It would take too long to explain many of them here. Two will serve as examples:

This sign is a "flat": ♭ Placed before a note, it indicates that the pitch of that note should be lowered by a half tone. (On the piano, a half tone is the distance from one key to the next, black or white.) The flat sign looks something like a small *b*, and that is what it used to be. It was placed on a B-line to show that the pitch of the B should be lowered by a half tone. Later, it was used for lowering the pitch of any note.

To raise the pitch a half tone, this sign was employed: ♯ . It is called a sharp, and it raises the pitch of any note a half tone.

The signs in this chapter are all practical ones. To appreciate this fact, all we need do is try to imagine how we could manage without them, or, in the case of music signs, how the musician could manage without them. Most of these signs help people to carry on the everyday business of living, anywhere in the world.

5/

Signs and Symbols in Religion and Magic

From the very beginning, people have found that some things cannot be expressed in words. Early people could not put into words their feeling of wonder at the world around them. It seemed a miracle that the sun came up each morning. When the full moon poured down its strange light from the night sky, this seemed even more of a miracle.

There were other mysteries too wonderful for words. There was the water in a river, flowing on and on forever. There was the wide blue sky overhead, and there was the night sky with its countless stars. There was the earth beneath man's feet, the trees and bushes and good grain that grew out of this earth.

Early people could not explain these things. And they could not express in words their feeling that life had a meaning beyond the everyday things they could see and touch. Nor could they draw pictures of feelings. But, as time went on, they began to draw various designs to express their feelings about themselves and their place in the world.

People chose the shapes that somehow felt right. They drew circles, squares, triangles, in a variety of patterns. These became symbols that stood for wonderful and unknown meanings. As the symbols became familiar to many people, they communicated their meanings.

The most important shape of all was the circle. There have always been circles in nature. Circle after circle spreads out when you drop a pebble into still water. Circles of growth inside a tree trunk are revealed when the tree is cut down.

Almost everywhere in the world, at some time long ago, people drew circles to represent the sun. We call the earliest ones sun wheels. They might be called pictures of the sun, but they were more than that. People worshiped the sun. To them it was a god. The bright round disk that they saw in the sky brought light and warmth to the earth—it seemed to be the source of life itself. Sun wheels often represented, not just the sun, but also life going on without end, as the circle has no end.

Here is an early drawing of the sun:

Sun wheels took various forms. As in other early drawings, certain designs were repeated over and over again, until a particular one began to have a similar meaning for many people. The meaning was not exactly the same for everyone because the design was not a picture of a thing or even of an idea. But most people felt much the same way about it.

The sun was worshiped in many different parts of the world. The Incas in South America believed that the god of the sun owned the earth. The sun god was one of the most important of the many gods of the Egyptians, who called him Ra. The disk of the sun appeared often in Egyptian carvings and paintings.

As we have seen, the hieroglyph for the sun was a dot in the middle of a circle: ⊙ This was also the Chinese sign for the sun. The same sign was used in ancient times in England, in Central America, by the Aztecs in Mexico, and in South America. It was the American Indian sign for "spirit." Sometimes the sign looked like this:

The Chinese, the Egyptians, the Aztecs, the American Indians, and others who used this sign lived far apart in time and place. And yet this and some of the other signs they invented were much the same. Perhaps the similarity came about because people everywhere in the world have some of the same feelings about themselves and the world they live in.

A circle with a cross inside it, like the spokes of a wheel, was used as a sun symbol long ago by people in the Far East and in northern Europe. It has been found in prehistoric cave paintings.

To the ancient Greeks, the sun wheel was also the wheel of a golden chariot. There was a Greek myth in which this chariot was driven across the sky each day by the sun god Apollo.

There have been other interesting circles representing the sun. Here are a few of them:

This is the sun with three rays. The bars at the ends of the rays represent the sky. Another symbol showed the sun with more rays:

another ancient sun wheel

*evening: the setting sun,
going down*

*morning: the rising sun,
going up*

A circle did not always represent the sun. This one is a snake biting its own tail:

A circle did not always represent the sun. This one is a snake biting its own tail:

The snake or serpent in a circle represents life beginning afresh. The snake himself seems to start life over again whenever he changes his skin. In Egypt, the snake in a circle represented the circle of the universe or the path of the sun god.

Here is still another circle, made by the Mayas in Central America. It represents God, the universe, and five mysteries.

A circle can be drawn in a spiral, like this:

A spiral often represented the earth, or nature struggling to create all the growing things on earth. Stretched out, it could reach from earth to heaven.

Here is a spiral that was carved on a rock in very early times in the West Indies; it represents the moon:

Like the sun wheels, these spirals meant more to people than just a line going around and around. It was hard to say in words what they meant. But when some people looked thoughtfully at a spiral, it made them feel that they too were a part of nature. They too were growing, struggling to understand the world around them.

An ancient Chinese symbol in a circle looked like this:

This symbol may look to us like two commas, or two tadpoles, but it had great meaning for the Chinese people. The light or *yang* part of the circle was white. The dark or *yin* part was black. The *yang-yin* circle represented the meaning of the universe itself. The *yang* part was considered the active or heavenly power in the universe. The light in the world comes from this power. So does fire. *Yang*, said the Chinese, is the sunny south side of a mountain. It is the north bank of a river because on a sunny day the river looks bright if you look at it from the north.

The *yin* part of the circle was thought to be the passive or earthy power in the universe. From this came darkness, shadow, and water. *Yin* is the shady north side of a mountain. It is the south bank of a river because on a sunny day the river looks dark from the south.

Yang is the warmth of the sun. *Yin* is the coolness of the shade. Both are a part of all life here on earth. Each can change into the other, as summer changes into winter, and day into night.

The ancient philosophers who designed the *yang-yin* symbol knew that very few things in the world are all light or all dark, all shady or all sunny. So they made a little dot of the white *yang* color in the black *yin* part of the circle. And they made a little dot of the black *yin* color in the white *yang* part of the circle.

This Chinese symbol represents all the things in the world that are opposites: light-dark, life-death, heat-cold, and so on. It represents the belief of the ancient philosophers that life was created out of these opposites working together. It is also a pleasing design. The flag of South Korea carries this symbol in blue and red on a white background. Look for it also on Chinese bowls and vases and other works of art.

The Mitsu Tomoe is a Japanese circle-symbol representing the universe revolving. This symbol has three comma-shaped designs:

Other circular designs have been used by thoughtful people in many parts of the world. Contemplating such designs has helped people to understand that their own thoughts and feelings are a part of the life of the whole world.

In India, a design known as a *yantra* is used for meditating about life. It is made up of a circle combined with triangles and other shapes.

Christian painters often put a halo around the heads of holy people in their pictures. The halo too is a circle. Circles were also built into churches. There is no more inspiring circle than a rose window, made of many-colored glass, in a great cathedral.

In Asia, the followers of Buddha have a symbol that is a wheel with eight spokes, indicating the eightfold path they believe people should follow. The idea of this wheel of the law has been traced back to the early sun wheels.

Today, most of us have lost sight of the original meaning of circles and other symbols. We do not worship the sun. But these figures can still have meaning for us. Circles and other symbols are used in modern painting. They have always been a part of the language used by artists to communicate their ideas and feelings to other people.

The painting by Paul Klee opposite the title page of this book, with the title "Secret Script Picture," is made up of graphic symbols. The picture by Kandinsky on the next page is all circles.

And here is an "op art" circle. What does this mean to you?

When a young child paints a circle, he moves his whole arm around, feeling the circle while he paints it. He is mak-

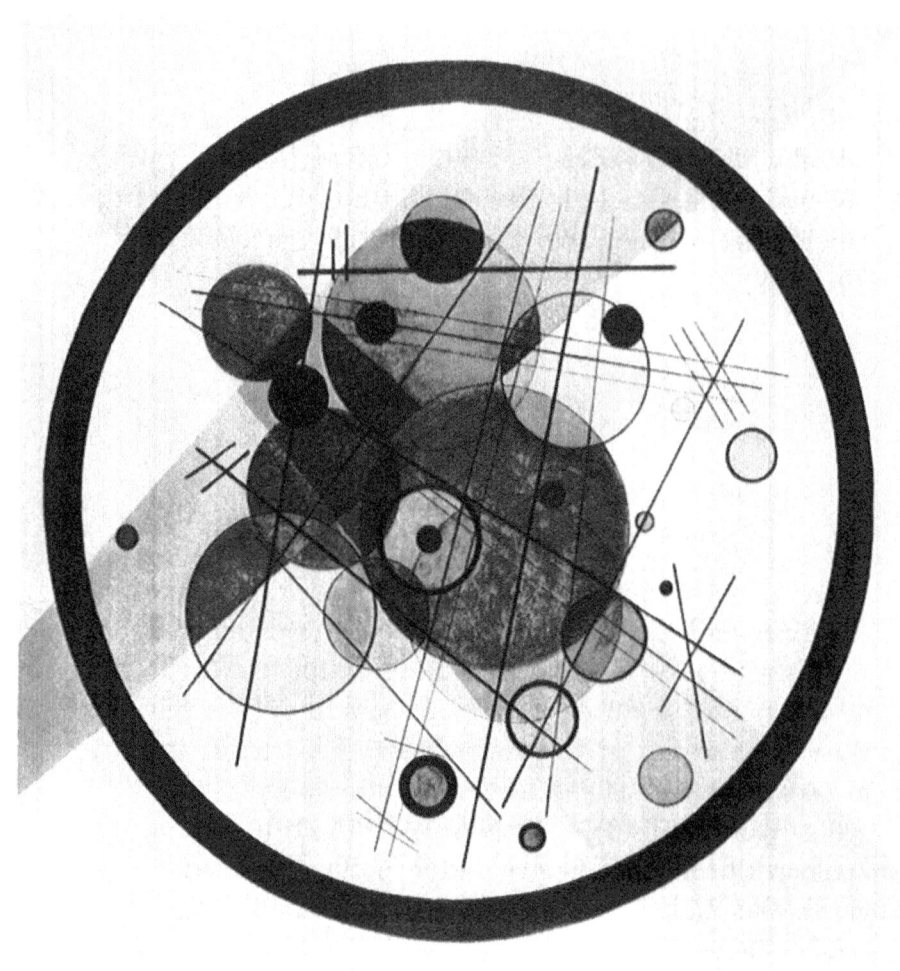

Circles In a Circle by Wassily Kandinsky

ing a symbol that is ages old. Perhaps some inkling of this
is buried deep within him.

People in ancient times thought a great deal about how
the world came to be. In the Far East, Hindu philosophers
reached the conclusion that the universe and everything in
it were made up of five great elements: earth, water, fire,
air, and the ether (which might be called outer space).

painting by a four-year-old

Everything in nature, they thought, was a combination of these elements. Earth itself was formed from them. Man too was made of a particular combination of these elements.

Each of the five elements was symbolized by a certain shape. According to this system of thought, the circle represented water—an idea quite different from its use as a sun wheel. Among these people water was thought to represent life and man's feeling about life.

The Hindu philosophers represented earth by a square.

This was placed at the bottom of a design that showed all the elements together. Water came next, then a right-side-up triangle for fire. Air was a crescent. The ether was given a shape that pointed up, into space. Its place was at the top of the design, which was called a *stupa*:

Chinese philosophers also believed in five elements, but theirs were earth, wood, metal, fire, and water. The ancient Greeks, on the other hand, thought that the world was made up of four elements: fire, air, earth, and water. Here is a symbol representing the four:

All these shapes had different meanings at different times and for different people. One symbol for water was a triangle pointing down, as water pours down. When this was combined with the triangle for fire, another design resulted, meaning fire and water.

Signs and symbols like these were an important means of communication. They were not aimless designs. To countless numbers of people they conveyed a meaning that could not be put into words. If they had merely been thought up by one individual making designs for fun with a pen or brush or knife, we would never hear about them today.

We usually think of the cross as a Christian symbol, but it was an important symbol for many people before there was a Christian religion. The cross as a symbol may have existed even before man learned to paint and carve. One stick made a line. Another stick laid across the first one made a cross. Perhaps the earliest cross was made of two crossed sticks that were used for making fire. This sign pointed in four directions, indicating the whole world. So, too, people looked everywhere as they tried to understand the meaning of the world. A line around the ends of the cross made a circle.

In early times, the cross and the sun wheel were both used in the worship of the sun. The cross could also mean the four parts of the world, the four winds that bring rain, or the four elements the world was supposed to be made of.

Here is a cross that was painted on a pebble in prehistoric times. It was found in the south of France:

In ancient Egypt the cross took various forms. In paintings, it was sometimes a bird with wings spread wide or a man with arms outstretched. As a hieroglyph, it might be one of the following:

$$\times \quad + \quad \mathsf{T}$$

The most famous Egyptian cross, however, was the *ankh*:

To the Egyptians, this sign meant "life" and "man" and sometimes the "universe" itself. The same design has been found in India and in Central and South America.

Though the cross meant somewhat different things to different people in ancient times, it was always a sign of strength and happiness, a sign of continuing life. It was a simple thing, easy to draw, and yet it was a symbol of hope to millions of people.

The swastika is another kind of cross, formed from the sun wheel by breaking the circle:

Originally, the swastika was a joyful sign for good luck. It is still known to Buddhists and other people in the Far East. In India, the arms of the swastika may point to the right or the left, clockwise or counterclockwise. With clockwise arms, it is considered a masculine sign, leading to the outer world. Counterclockwise arms make it a feminine sign, leading to the inner mind of man.

The American Indians had their own swastika, with arms pointing counterclockwise. In Mexico, an elaborate calendar was worked out in the shape of a swastika.

The American Indians knew the symbol of the cross long before they heard of the Christian religion. Here is a cross of the Dakotas, Sioux Indians who lived on the Great Plains. It was designed to be worn on the front of the body:

This cross represented the four winds. The top was the cold and powerful north wind. The foot of the cross was the fiery south wind. The left arm of the cross (on the right in the drawing) was to cover the heart. This was the east wind, representing life and love. The right arm (on the left in the drawing) was the gentle west wind, blowing from the land of spirit. The center represented earth and man, influenced all through life by the gods and the winds. As we have seen, the Indians also used this sign for "spirit."

To Christians, the cross is a symbol of the hope for a better life that Christ brought to the world. The Christian cross has many forms. Here are some of the best-known:

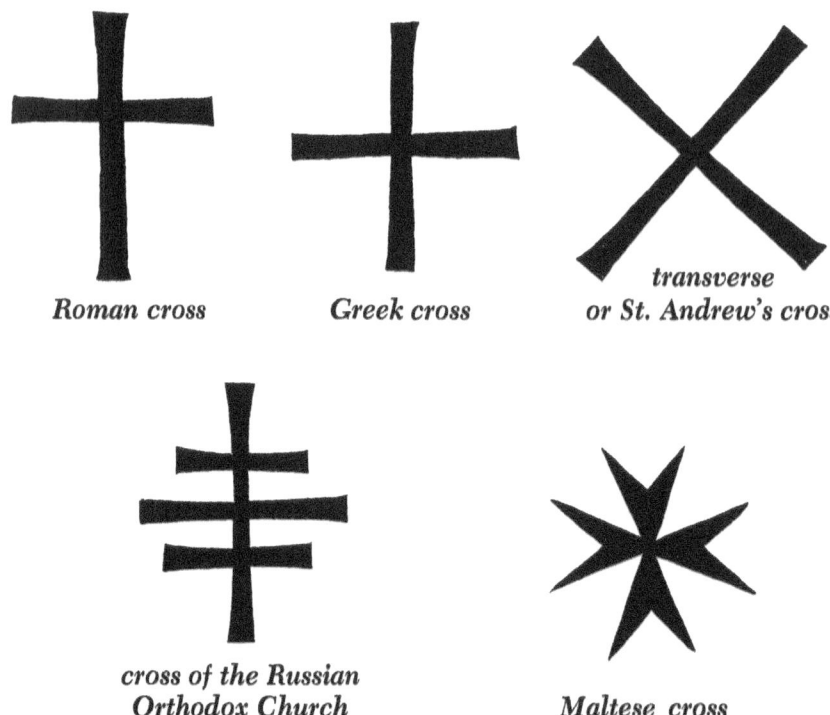

Roman cross *Greek cross* *transverse or St. Andrew's cross*

cross of the Russian Orthodox Church *Maltese cross*

Many signs used in the Western Hemisphere are based on the Roman cross. Some of these were considered monograms of Christ. Here is a well-known monogram:

This monogram probably developed from an ancient oriental symbol for the rising sun, showing the sun over a cross representing its rays, like this:

The Roman emperor Constantine, who was a Christian, had this monogram embroidered in gold on his purple banner when he went to war. To him, it meant the first two letters of the name of Christ in Greek: X and P, *chi* and *rho*.

There are other uses of the cross as a symbol. It is the signature of people who cannot write. In mathematics, it is the plus sign or, turned sideways, the multiplication sign. Crosses at the end of a letter mean "love and kisses": X X X. On the other hand, a skull with crossed bones underneath it warns of poison or danger.

The earliest symbol of the Christian church was the fish. Because the Christian religion was outlawed by the Roman government, the meaning of the fish was a carefully kept secret, known only to Christians. The first letters of each word of a Greek phrase meaning "Jesus Christ, Son of God, Saviour" make the word *ichthys*, Greek for "fish." The fish also represented a living being in the water of life. It was food for the life of man, there for the taking.

Here is an early Christian drawing of a fish, with the Greek letters:

All the religions of the world have their own symbols. As we have seen, Christianity has its cross, Buddhism its wheel of the law. The six-pointed star formed from two overlapping triangles is a symbol of the Jewish religion. It is called the "Star of David."

A six-pointed star was also the famous seal with which King Solomon, in the Old Testament of the Bible, was said to have worked miracles.

The World Council of Churches, an organization of 217 Orthodox, Anglican, and Protestant churches, has adopted as its emblem an old symbol of the church, a ship in which the faithful are carried over the sea of life. The mast and the yardarm of the ship form a cross. The letters above the ship, OIKOUMENE, spell the Greek word meaning "the inhabited world." The Council helps Christians to come to know each other and work together, throughout "the inhabited world."

Many other symbols have been important in religion. Some of these are things rather than graphic signs, just as the cross can be a thing rather than a sign. The tree was a symbol of growing life and of hope. Mountains suggested mystery and power. To the ancient Greeks, a mountain was the home of the gods.

Some of the ancient symbols from which Chinese writing developed were religious symbols. Here is the Chinese character for "eternity," time going on forever:

永

This symbol is a picture of rivers, water flowing on and on, with a short stroke at the top to lift the meaning beyond the everyday world. It is a lovely design, quite apart from its meaning.

Religious symbols have been used in a great variety of ways. In eastern Asia, north of China, the Tartars and Mongols used to draw religious symbols on their drum tops. Combined with the sound of the drums, different designs were said to produce different effects, through a kind of religious magic. In some designs, we again find the circle with a dot in the center ⊙ representing the sun or the moon.

Here is a design from one drum top: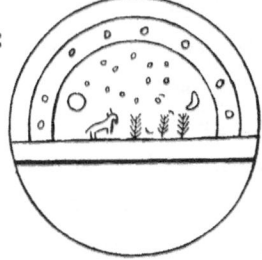

The outer rim (with nothing drawn in it) represents heaven. Under that there is a dotted rainbow, and under that the stars. To the left of the stars is the sun, and on the right, a crescent moon. The other figures are a goat and three trees.

This is a kind of picture of the world, with the heavens above, the earth at the center, and the underworld below, with no drawing in it. It is a symbolic picture that could convey its meaning only to those who already understood the signs that were used. The spirits who controlled the Mongol world were supposed to understand.

The sound of some drums was wild and upsetting. The sound of others was so soothing that the Mongols believed it had the power to make sick people feel well again.

Signs and symbols have been used for magic, too. One such sign represents an eye. In ancient Egypt this one was supposed to bring good health:

Often the eye was believed to protect a person or a thing. An eye would be painted on the prow of a ship to guard against shipwreck. This is still done in some places. Or the image of an eye might be painted on a fragile bowl or cup to protect it from breakage.

Here is a symbol that represented the open eye of God, perhaps derived from the earlier sun circles:

In some churches, a picture representing the eye of God was painted on the wall at the front of the church, to watch over all the people.

Signs used for magic have taken many forms. In Japan, a design showing a crane was supposed to bring good luck. A turtle was for long life.

Magic signs can also be made just for fun. In eastern Europe, Easter eggs are decorated with gay patterns in the spring. Each design has a meaning that has been the same for countless years. A flower means love. A pine tree is for health. A spiral is for growing. Hens and roosters mean that wishes will come true.

From the very beginning, there was thought to be magic in writing. Almost all early writing included circles in various ways. The following designs, and many others, have been found in prehistoric and ancient writing:

Ancient people told stories about how the art of writing was given to man by the gods. The Egyptians said that writing was invented by the god Thoth, who had the head of the ibis, a sacred bird. He scratched his bill on the shores of the Nile, and that was the first writing. Thoth was pictured with a reed brush and ink palette for writing.

The Romans attributed their alphabet to a god named Mercury. In India, the Hindu god Brahma was said to have introduced letters when he needed them for writing down his teachings. It was believed that he traced the first Hindu characters in leaves of gold.

The earliest written alphabet of the northern European people called Teutons was made up of characters called runes. The word "rune" itself means "secret." Runes date far back in history.

Runic letters consisted entirely of straight lines because they were scratched or carved. They were often used for magic—both good and evil, it was said. They were carved on tools and weapons and on stones, wherever good luck might be needed.

Runes carved on a staff were supposed to cure disease. An arrow pointing up ↑ was for victory in battle. An ✗ would protect one against a poisoned cup. In fact, a cup filled with a poisoned drink would upset itself if the runes scratched on it were lucky. The sign ▶ was supposed to make an enemy go mad.

A runic magician named Egill was said to have discovered that a certain maiden's sickness was caused by runes scratched in the stone floor beneath her couch. Egill dug the stones up and replaced them with stones carved with lucky runes. Presumably the maiden was cured.

Runic characters were also inscribed on mountains, on the face of rocks, on coins, and on jewelry. The Norsemen said that their god Odin had invented the runes. It is many years now since they have been used at all.

All the symbols we have been talking about in this chapter do much more than convey information to people. They are an attempt to put into visible form ideas and feelings that cannot themselves be seen. Symbols such as these have helped man over the long centuries to understand the meaning of his world.

6/

Ownership
Marks
and
Trademarks

Another kind of sign that has been important all through history is the mark that means ownership, or identification. Trademarks are identification marks, but they are by no means the only ones.

Put into words, an identification mark or trademark might say, "These bricks were made by Ahmenhop," or "This cow belongs to Sam Busby's Ranch," or "These crackers were made by the Truffler Biscuit Company." Like other signs, an identification mark can be understood at a glance by anyone who is familiar with its meaning, no matter what language he speaks.

Simple designs have been found scratched on tools and weapons from very early times. Early man made these tools and weapons himself, chipping away, little by little, at stone or wood or bone. He must have wanted to make sure that everyone knew they were his.

Trademarks were widely used in ancient Egypt and Mesopotamia. Potters scratched their own marks on the pots they made. Brick makers marked their bricks. Here are some early marks made by masons on the buildings they constructed of bricks:

In ancient Rome, tiles and bricks had marks that showed which factory made them, what kiln they were fired in, and which contractor was to use them in a building.

In ancient Egypt, the monuments and buildings erected during a particular sovereign's reign were marked with his identification sign. Sometimes these signs were monograms, designs made up of some or all of the letters of the ruler's name. Queen Cleopatra's monogram was a cartouche, an oval containing the hieroglyphic letter-signs that spelled out her name. The decoration varied, but the letters and the oval enclosing them were always the same. Probably even Egyptians who could not read most of the hieroglyphs would recognize the queen's monogram when they saw it.

In medieval times, noble families identified themselves by a coat of arms. These colorful designs were based on an elaborate system of symbols. There were lions for bravery, leopards for watchfulness and cunning, as well as eagles, peacocks, roses and other flowers, stars, and many other symbolical figures. No two families had the same coat of arms.

Such identification was needed in medieval days. Knights wore armor with helmets over their faces and carried shiny shields. One knight looked very much like the next one, and so it became the practice for a knight to have his own mark blazoned on his shield, as an identification. Later, when soldiers no longer carried shields, the coats of arms were engraved on silver dishes and other utensils or placed over the doors of houses, for decoration as much as for identification.

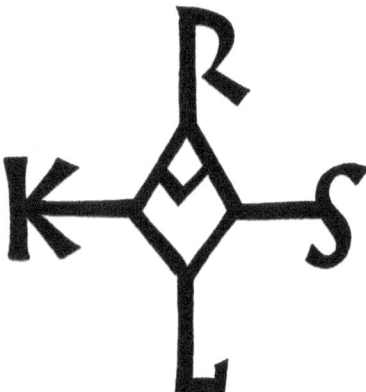

In addition to coats of arms, kings had their own individual monograms. This one belonged to the French king Charlemagne:

Ordinary people in medieval times also had special marks for identifiying their possessions and themselves, though these were neither monograms nor coats of arms. Marks used to show ownership were called house-marks or holdings-marks. These marks were clipped out of the hairy coats of horses and painted on the fleece of sheep. They were plowed into the surface of fields, carved on trees, embroidered on rugs and clothing. A man's tools had his own mark punched into the iron or burned onto the wooden handle. Sometimes domestic animals were branded with a hot iron.

Here is an early house-mark carved on a stick:

Later, the house-mark was used to identify the members of a family. Still later, some of the same signs turned up as trademarks or the marks of craftsmen and artists.

The following are examples of simple family signs:

These were usually carved on wood. That is why they have no curves. Curves came later, when some signs were drawn or painted.

Some family signs had particularly interesting shapes. Here are a few. Their names may have been given to them after they were made, simply because they looked like a specific object.

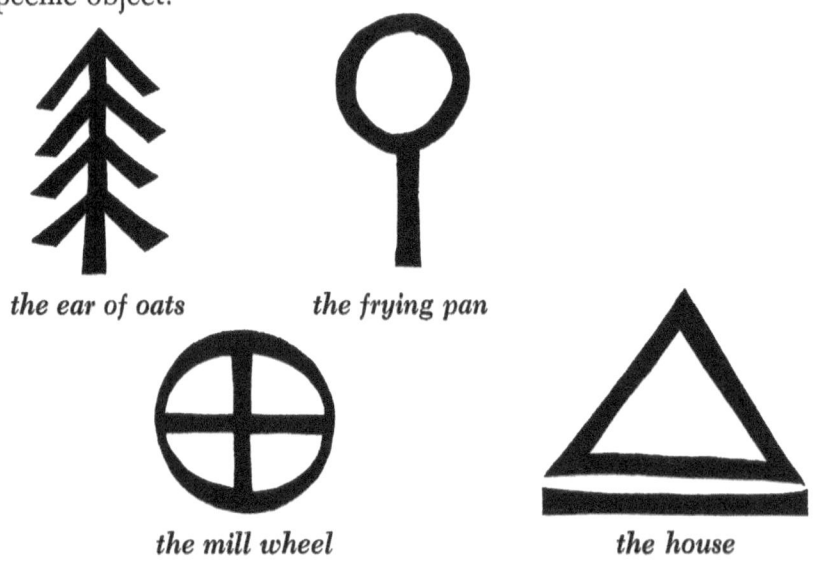

the ear of oats   *the frying pan*

the mill wheel   *the house*

The following are the signs of a man, his brother, and his son, all based on a mushroom:

Some of the old house-marks belonged to individuals or families who become famous. This one belonged to the artist and engineer Michelangelo:

Here is an old sign used to represent a city on a map. It looks like a walled city of the Middle Ages.

After the city had been destroyed, it was shown like this on later maps:

Many Indian tribes in North America chose an animal as a totem, or symbol, for identification. Families had their own totem animals, too. A totem animal was thought to be a blood relative of the family or tribe. On the northwest coast of this continent, Indians decorated the sides of their dwellings and their towering totem poles with their own totem animals.

As time went on, special marks were used for many occupations. Some of them had been house-marks. Others were newly designed. Merchants identified the goods they sold with their own marks. Papermakers had marks for identifying their paper. Goldsmiths and printers had special marks.

Stonemasons had always carved their marks on their work. Here are two marks that were carved on stone in Roman times:

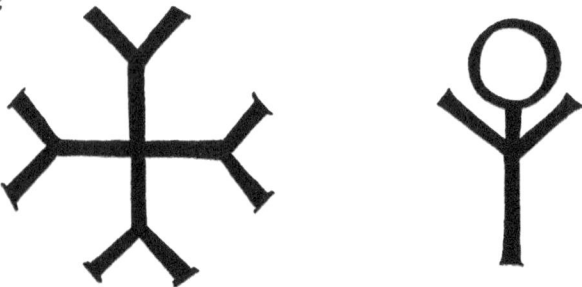

Signs carved by masons in medieval times can still be seen on cathedrals and other buildings in Europe. These were often quite ingenious. Here are three:

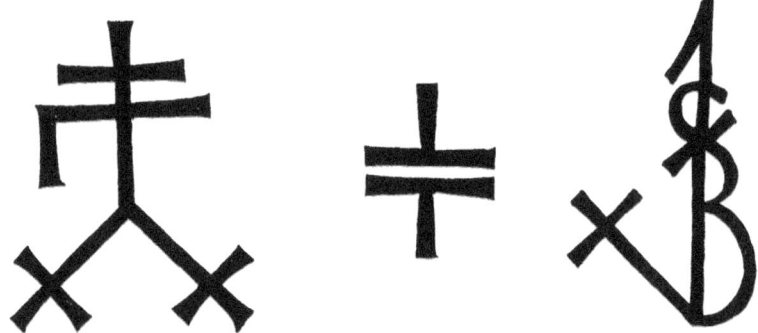

Printers and publishers have had their own marks since books were first printed by a press instead of being lettered by hand. (This momentous change took place in the second half of the fifteenth century in Europe.) At the end of a book, the printer would give information about the process he had used in printing it. He followed this with his own trademark, called a colophon.

The famous Italian printer Aldus Manutius was one of the first to publish books at a price many people could afford.

His aim was to make the classics of Greek literature available to all the people. (It was he, you will remember, who adapted Greek punctuation marks to his printing.) At the end of each of the books Aldus Manutius published, this colophon appeared:

Present-day publishers no longer print their mark at the end of each book, but some do have trademarks.

Other professions and occupations have their own marks. The familiar symbol for a medical doctor is the caduceus:

The word "caduceus" comes from the Greek word meaning a "herald's wand" or "staff." The symbol itself is a very old one. It was used in India in ancient times and has also been traced to early Mesopotamia.

In ancient Greece, the caduceus was the wand of Mercury, messenger of the gods and god of dreams, magic, and trade. Throughout the centuries, it appeared on printers'

signs, on merchant ships, and as an emblem of secret socie-
ties. It was finally chosen as a medical symbol in England
at the time of King Henry the Eighth, in the sixteenth century.

The serpent in ancient times meant wisdom, health, and
long life. It was considered to be the most powerful symbol
against disease because the serpent seems to renew itself
each time it grows a new skin and sheds its old one.

The caduceus has two intertwining serpents twisted
around an upright wand, with two wings at the top. There
is a similar symbol with just one serpent, the staff of Aesculapius, ancient Greek and Roman god of healing. Aesculapius was said to have been followed by a serpent as he
went about performing cures.

The staff of Aesculapius, transposed on the sign of the
United Nations, is the symbol of the World Health Organization.

On the wide rangelands in the United States, cattle brands
are well-known marks of identification. In branding, the
owner's identification mark is burned into the hide of an
animal. The process was not invented here. It has a long
history.

Branding was done in Egypt about 4,000 years ago. Drawings and hieroglyphic writing on the walls of Egyptian tombs show how cattle were branded at that time. Later, in France, horses that were hired out were branded with the owner's mark.

Branding was introduced to North America by the Spanish. In the sixteenth century, the explorer Cortez brought his family brand to Mexico. It had a design of three crosses. Other Spaniards brought their own marks, and their descendants continued the practice of branding. A Spanish brand was often taken from the family coat of arms, which might have been used for centuries in Spain.

Cattlemen north of the Mexican border soon saw how practical branding could be. There were no fences on the range in the early days of this country. One steer or cow looked much like the next one, and there was no way at all for a cattleman to prove that he owned a particular cow, or even a whole herd. The problem was too often settled with blazing guns. Branding was a better way. On the open range, anyone could see that a steer with a Lazy-H brand on it did not belong to the same ranch as one with a Walking Tadpole brand.

At first, branding presented some complicated problems. Sometimes several cattlemen chose the same brand. In time, laws were made requiring all brands to be registered with the state government, and prohibiting any duplication of designs. After that, the main problem for a new cattleman was thinking up a brand that had not already been used. The law against duplication resulted in a great variety of brands coming into use—Crossed W, Crow-Foot, Swan, Swinging Diamonds, to name a few.

Branding has a language all its own that is read in a particular way. Letters are sometimes used in cattle brands, but they are usually just part of the design, not parts of words. Brands are read from left to right, top to bottom, and from outside in. Thus, **Ⓑ** is the Circle B.

Letters turned sideways or upside down in cattle brands take on new meanings. A letter tipped over slightly is "tumbling." Lying down flat, it is "lazy." Legs added to a letter make it "walking," and so on.

Here are a few examples of old-time brands:

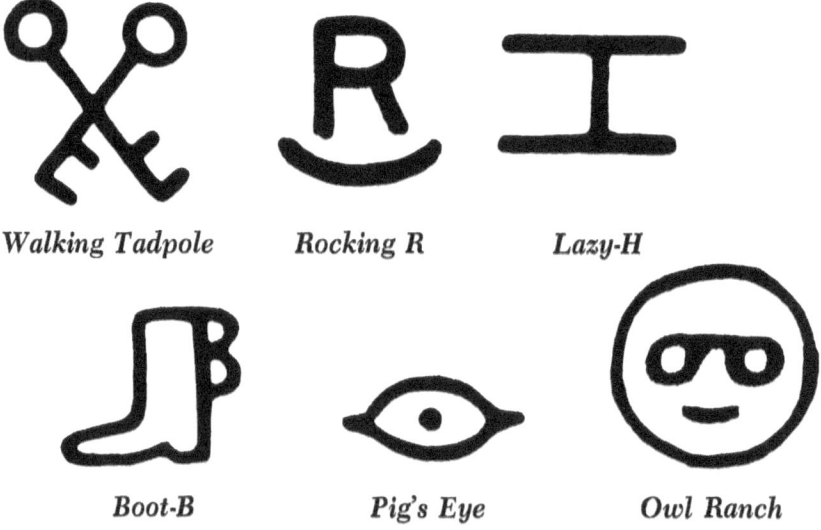

Walking Tadpole   *Rocking R*   *Lazy-H*

Boot-B   *Pig's Eye*   *Owl Ranch*

In the early days, when logging first became a big business in the United States, it was easy to confuse one lumber company's logs with another's. This was especially likely to happen while the freshly cut logs were lying in the forest and, later, when they were being floated down rivers. Consequently, logs were marked for identification. Some of these marks resemble cattle brands. Others are quite different.

Countries have identification marks, too. Each country has its own Great Seal for use on official documents. And each country has its own flag.

Flags are important to all countries today, but the use of the flag as a national symbol does not date far back in history. The earliest ancestors of the flag were, perhaps, tribal symbols in the form of carved birds or animals that were mounted on a staff and carried into battle.

A square of fringed cloth hanging from a crossbar on a spear was carried by the Roman cavalry in ancient times. Sometimes designs were put on the cloth. This was a kind of flag.

In the Middle Ages, religious symbols were carried on banners. Knights sometimes had their coats of arms embroidered on their own flags. But the use of a flag to represent a whole nation came later. It developed only when a symbol was needed to express the love people had for their own country.

The thirteen stripes of our flag symbolize the original thirteen colonies; the fifty stars are for the fifty states. But the flag means much more than this to the citizens of the United States. It represents the ideals the country stands for —"liberty and justice for all."

Suppose you wanted to have an identification mark for yourself, your family, or your club. You could design one. It could be anything you like, but it would have to be simple and striking if you wanted other people to remember it as yours. You would do well to base your design on a circle, square, or triangle.

Another way to get an identification mark would be to choose an old one that appealed to you. There are books of old signs, some of them listed in the bibliography at the end of this book.

Individual people and organizations have, at times, chosen old signs as their identification marks. Here is a sign that appears on the covers of books by the British author W. Somerset Maugham:

Mr. Maugham had this sign placed outside the gate that led to his villa in the South of France, and over the front door. He had it printed on his writing paper too. It was his mark.

The Maugham sign is an old one that was brought from Mauretania, in French West Africa, by Mr. Maugham's father. It was supposed to provide protection against the Evil Eye, which otherwise might do great harm. Just what the sign represents is not known. It may be a symbol of an upright sword piercing through darkness into light, which is represented by the arch of the sky. Or, the lines within the arch may be a cross.

One organization that has adapted an old sign as its identification mark is The Experiment in International Living. The Experiment, in its own words, is "devoted to creating mutual respect and understanding among the different peoples of the world." It sends American college and high school students abroad for eight weeks in the summer and, at the same time, brings foreign students to the United States. During half of this period, the student visits with a family. Lasting friendships are formed; understanding grows.

The Experiment wanted a sign that would express the idea of people living together, and of human life going on forever, from one generation to the next. They chose the knot symbol and developed it into this sign:

The founder of The Experiment found the symbol quite by chance, on a piece of old iron in an antique shop in Austria. It appealed to him at once, and he determined to find out all he could about it. By reading books and by consulting experts who knew a great deal about old signs, he learned that the knot symbol had a long and interesting history. With many variations, it dates back to the time of Stone Age man, before there was any written history.

The knot symbol was also found in India, in ancient Persia, in Egypt, and in various European countries. A number of different religions used it. In Egypt, it was almost as important as the cross to a group of early Christians called Copts. The Coptic Christians in Ethiopia, south of Egypt, still use it today.

Moslems also have a form of the knot. In a still different form, it is known to Buddhists in India, China, and Japan.

It was even found among the Indians who lived in the south-western part of our country before the time of Columbus.

The meaning of the knot sign varied, but it usually had to do with the continuity of life, the idea that life in the human family goes on and on, from one generation to the next, without end. Twisting and turning, the lines in the knot symbol also go on without end.

People no longer know what some of the variations of the knot sign meant. They do know that the knot was sometimes used as a magic sign against evil.

Here is an example of the knot symbol that appeared on the keystone of a small archway in the old town of Rothenburg, Germany:

This one was on the capital of a column in a Christian church, as a sign against evil:

The Buddhist form of the knot, called "The Mystic Diagram," had six loops instead of four. It was supposed to be the thread that guides the thoughtful man to happiness, and was also a good luck sign, for long life.

The following knot symbol appears in an old Japanese family emblem:

Like The Experiment in International Living, numerous other organizations that bring people together have their own emblems. Often these include the initials of the organization, or its complete name. Usually, the design for a particular organization is made especially for that group, though sometimes symbols from the past are used. The 4-H Club emblem is a green four-leaf clover, for good luck. The H's stand for head, heart, hands, and health.

Present-day trademarks are almost always specially designed. Trademarks are a kind of picture writing. They tell us more quickly than words, "This program comes to you from the Columbia Broadcasting Company," or, "This company's products are made from trees."

Most trademark designs are based on such basic shapes as circles, triangles, and squares. The way these are used depends to a large extent on the product or the purpose of the company. The designer tries to combine shapes in a simple pattern that people will recognize at once as belonging to the organization or the product. The design must also be one that can easily be recognized when reduced to a very small size.

Now for some examples—first, trademarks of manufacturers. The three following trademarks belong to companies that make products from trees, such as lumber, pulp, and paper:

Weyerhaeuser Co.   *International Paper Co.*   *Boise Cascade*

Each of these trademarks uses an evergreen tree in a different way. Look for these marks on wood and paper products, such as plywood, milk containers, and cartons.

Manufacturers of cloth have special trademarks. Cloth-

PURE VIRGIN WOOL

ing made of fine wool that is approved by the Wool Bureau bears the above mark. It was chosen in a contest for an appropriate trademark held by the Wool Bureau, Inc. Designers from all over the world sent in drawings. The winning trademark was made by an Italian designer.

Materials made of Du Pont stretch nylon are advertised with this stretchy-looking trademark:

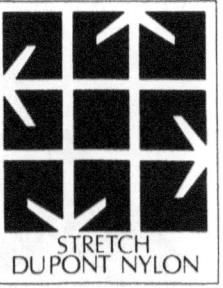

ISIS, an Italian company that makes waterproof goods, features this mark:

The National Biscuit Company calls its trademark the "coat of arms" of the Nabisco family. It is taken from an ancient symbol, the circle and cross with two bars, representing the creation of life. This mark was also used as a colophon by the Society of Printers in Venice, Italy, in the fifteenth century. Here is the old colophon:

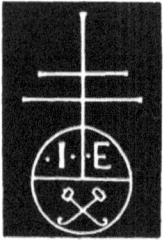

And here is the NABISCO trademark of today:

Trademarks can be registered with the United States Patent Office in Washington. Once a mark is registered, it cannot be used by another company or an individual. A trademark would be of little value to a company if anyone else could use it.

Organizations often have emblems that suggest their work. The Brooklyn Bureau of Social Service helps families in trouble, and so their emblem quite logically pictures a family:

The World Wildlife Fund uses the giant panda to symbolize its work of saving rare species and those that are in danger of becoming extinct. The panda itself is a rare animal that lives only in the bamboo forests in a small area of mountain country in Asia.

An emblem that represents people in a circle was the identifying sign for the Universal and International Exhibition in Montreal, Canada, in 1967 (EXPO67):

The theme of the exhibition was "Man and His World," and the emblem represents people coming together in friendship, all around the world.

The design comes from an ancient sign meaning "man"— a vertical line with outstretched arms: Ψ Two such signs with the arms linked mean "friendship": ΨΨ A circle of these suggests the world.

The work of some organizations cannot very well be shown in a trademark or emblem. This is true of banking. The Chase Manhattan Bank in New York City therefore decided to use a completely abstract design representing no actual object:

This design has a very positive meaning, however. A bank has separate departments for different kinds of business. The emblem, too, is a single unit made up of separate parts. The pointed tip of each part of the design conveys a feeling of motion, and that is appropriate because a bank is full of activity and purpose.

Though this design is clearly modern, its eight-sided shape suggests ancient coins, a suitable idea for a bank. Like all good trademarks and emblems, this one is simple, attractive, and easily remembered.

The Campaign for Nuclear Disarmament in England adopted this sign in 1958:

It represents the semaphore (flag signal) for the initials N and D. (N in semaphore = $\wedge$; D = $|$.) Combined, these shapes make the ancient sign for man—upside down. This means the death of man, which can be caused by nuclear weapons. The circle represents the unborn child, who also dies. Today people use this sign to express their desire for peace, or as a protest against whatever they feel is wrong with our society.

We have come a long way from a simple mark scratched on a tool to show ownership. But all identification marks say essentially the same thing: "This is mine—my family, my work, my business, my belief, my purpose in life."

7/

Signs
for Science
and
Industry

Scientists are using more signs and symbols today than ever before. Many of these are new. But science itself is not new; it is thousands of years old.

In ancient times, science was often mixed with philosophy. Science and philosophy are both ways of thinking about the world. As we have seen in Chapter 5, early philosophers came to the conclusion that the earth was formed from four or five simple substances called elements. Symbols were developed to represent these elements. This was a beginning of science.

The symbols for these elements were not always the same. Those used in the Middle Ages often differed from those used in ancient times. In ornamentation, such as wrought iron, the following symbols were sometimes employed:

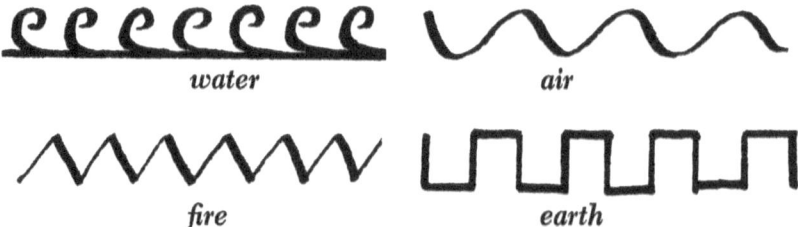

water   *air*

fire   *earth*

In the Middle Ages, the four elements were also represented by circle-symbols:

fire   *air*   *water*   *earth*

There was, it seems, no attempt to design symbols for use all over the world. Science was not thought of as a separate and precise division of knowledge, with its own special signs and symbols.

Astronomy is one of the oldest sciences in the world, perhaps the oldest. Long before there were telescopes for watching the stars, people scanned the heavens at night and watched the sun by day. They figured out the pattern of the waxing and waning of the moon and devised amazingly accurate calendars. All this information was acquired through observation with the naked eye.

Here are three signs used by early astronomers:

Venus   *Earth*   *Mercury*

Notice the circle and cross in these signs. As we saw before, they were early religious symbols. Astronomers' signs are said to have been first used by the ancient Egyptians.

Three more early signs for the planets:

| *Jupiter* | *Mars* | *Neptune* |

Jupiter, the king of the Roman gods, was associated with the moon. Mars was the Roman god of war. The symbol for Neptune represents the staff or trident that this Roman sea-god carried.

The early astronomers thought that the whole sky rotated around the earth. The sun, in addition to making the daily east-west rotation, also seemed to move in another circle, which took a year to complete. This circle was the center line of a path called the zodiac, made up of 12 groups of stars or constellations. In traveling this path, every 30 days the sun entered another constellation. The ancient people made signs to represent each of these groups of stars. The 12 signs are known as the signs of the zodiac:

Aquarius,
the water-bearer   *Pisces,*   *Aries,*
                                  the fishes   *the ram*

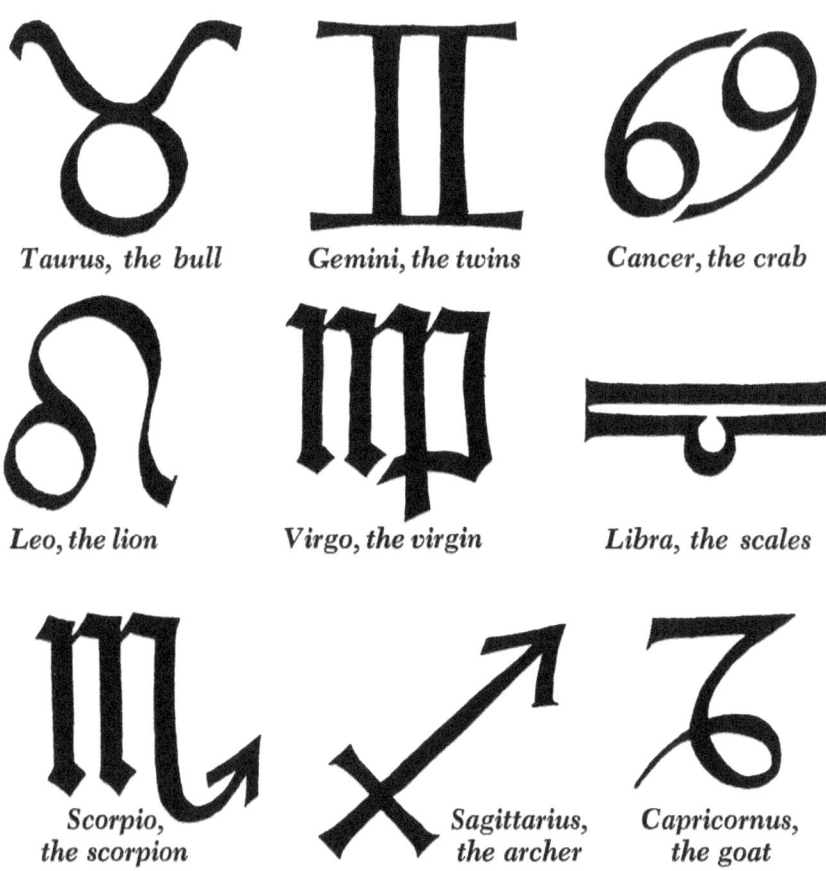

Taurus, the bull   Gemini, the twins   Cancer, the crab

Leo, the lion   Virgo, the virgin   Libra, the scales

Scorpio,   Sagittarius,   Capricornus,
the scorpion   the archer   the goat

These signs are not always represented in exactly this way. Sometimes they are represented by pictures showing a ram, fishes, a lion, twins, and so on.

Since early times, astrologers have used the signs of the zodiac in predicting the influence of the stars on human affairs.

Astronomers, who study the stars, and botanists, who study plants, have used signs on their charts and diagrams from the very beginning. Here are early astronomers' signs for the seasons of the year:

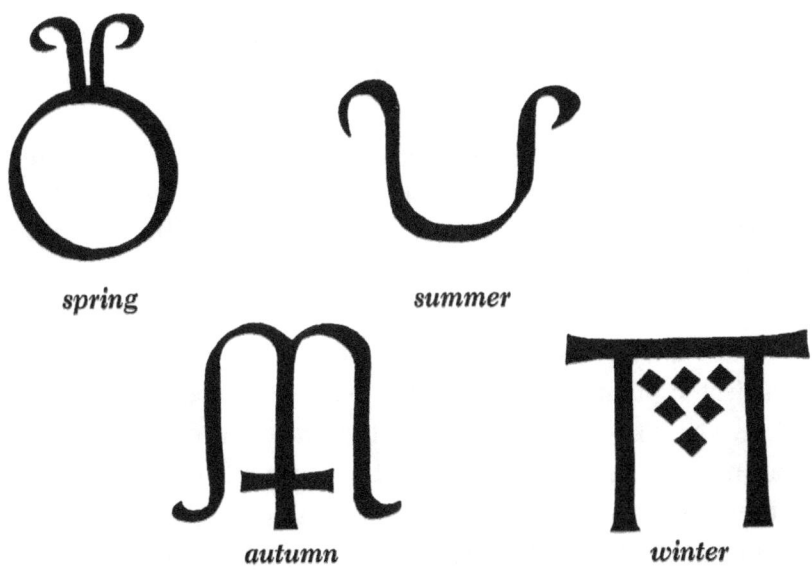

spring   *summer*

autumn   *winter*

Some of the early botanical signs are still in use today. These are just a few:

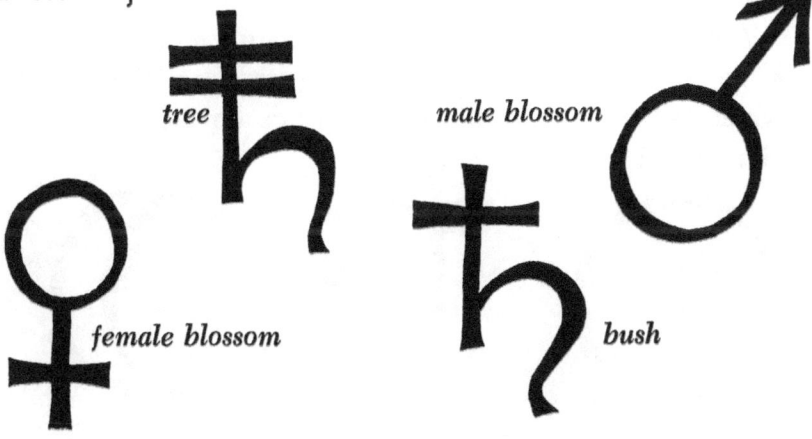

tree   *male blossom*

female blossom   *bush*

Note that the botanist's sign for male is also the astronomer's sign for the planet Mars, named for the Roman god of war. This is indeed an appropriate sign for male. The botanist's sign for female is the astronomer's sign for the planet Venus, named for the Roman goddess of love and beauty.

The same signs for male and female are used today, not only for plants, but also for indicating male and female birds or animals, especially in illustrations for scientific books.

Chemistry is the study of the composition of things. The earliest signs used in chemistry were designed several hundred years ago by the alchemists. These were men who experimented to see if they could make gold out of lead and other ordinary metals. At the same time they thought they were exploring the mysteries of the human mind. To guard their secrets, they invented their own special symbols. The secrets were so well kept that even today no one knows the meaning of some of the symbols.

A number of the alchemist's symbols for metals were the same as those used to represent the stars and the planets, which were thought to have influence on certain metals. Here are three of these:

gold, the sun   lead, Saturn   silver, the moon

Notice that the sign for gold is also the Egyptian hieroglyph for the sun.

Other early chemical signs were based on religious symbols. Many were remarkably beautiful. We can see that, for alchemists, these symbols held a meaning beyond their practical use.

Here are more of the alchemist's symbols:

olive oil	*antimony (a metal)*	*borax*
white lead	*arsenic*	*annealing*

(Annealing was the process of heating by which the alchemists sought to change metals.)

Most of the early chemical symbols are no longer in use. Instead, chemists today use combinations of letters as symbols for all the natural elements. Such a symbol is generally made up of the first letter, or the first and another letter, of the English, Latin, or German name of an element. For example, H stands for hydrogen, O for oxygen, Pb for lead (from its Latin name *plumbum*), Na for sodium (from the Latin *natrium*).

In practical use, these combinations of letters are as truly symbols as they would be if they were made up of abstract designs. They are understood by chemists all over the world, whatever their language.

These letter-symbols can be combined with numbers and other familiar signs to describe various combinations of the natural elements and the changes that take place in them. Here are some combinations:

H_2SO_4 (sulphuric acid)
H_2O (water)
NaCl (sodium chloride, our table salt)

And here is a typical chemical equation showing the change that takes place as two chemicals combine. It tells us that when one molecule of hydrogen combines with one of chlorine, the result is two molecules of hydrochloride.

$$H_2 + Cl_2 \longrightarrow 2HCl$$

Anyone who knows chemistry would understand this combination of signs. The student of chemistry must know the meaning of hundreds of such signs and combinations of signs so that he can communicate with other chemists. In fact, every branch of scientific knowledge has its own signs for communicating its own special kind of information. It would be impossible for everyone to understand all the signs in all the sciences. Nor do we need to.

Meteorology, the study of weather and weather forecasting, is a science with some fascinating symbols. In a daily newspaper, look at the weather report from the United States Department of Commerce Weather Bureau. At the bottom of the weather map is an explanation of all the symbols used on it. Some of these are pure symbols; some use letters. For example:

O clear weather   (r) rain

◑ partly cloudy   (s) snow

● cloudy   (t) thunderstorms

🌀 hurricane   (f) fog

To show the speed of the wind, a line like an arm or an arrow projects from the weather circle. The number of "feathers" or "flags" on this arm changes as the wind increases or decreases. Here are just a few of the possible variations:

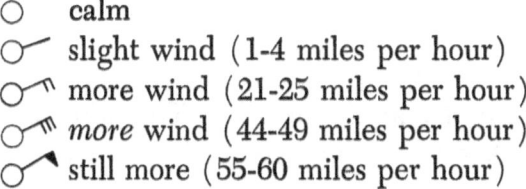

O   calm
O⁻ slight wind (1-4 miles per hour)
Oⁿ more wind (21-25 miles per hour)
Oⁿᵐ *more* wind (44-49 miles per hour)
O⁓ still more (55-60 miles per hour)

In addition to the signs on daily weather maps, meteorologists have a special symbolic code by which they can report the state of the weather. This is not a code just for the United States. Meteorologists all over the world use it, like an international language, to communicate with one another. The code makes it possible to send detailed reports about the weather to all parts of the world for the benefit of aircraft, ships at sea, and even astronauts planning a trip into outer space. Here are some random samples chosen because of their interesting designs, not for their importance as symbols:

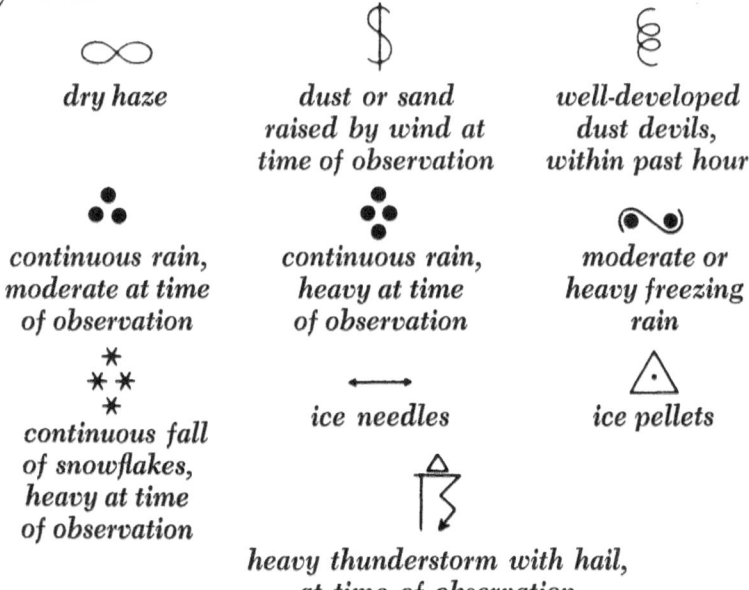

dry haze

dust or sand raised by wind at time of observation

well-developed dust devils, within past hour

continuous rain, moderate at time of observation

continuous rain, heavy at time of observation

moderate or heavy freezing rain

continuous fall of snowflakes, heavy at time of observation

ice needles

ice pellets

heavy thunderstorm with hail, at time of observation

Scientists have learned a great deal in recent years about that tiny particle of matter, the atom. The popular symbol for the atom is known all over the world:

Atomic scientists use many mathematical and scientific symbols in their work. With these they can communicate with one another. Here are some "doodles" made by a visiting scientist at Brookhaven National Laboratory. They represent his thinking as he discussed an important principle of nuclear physics with another scientist. The result—a new idea in atomic research. The doodles don't make sense to you? Then you are not an atomic scientist!

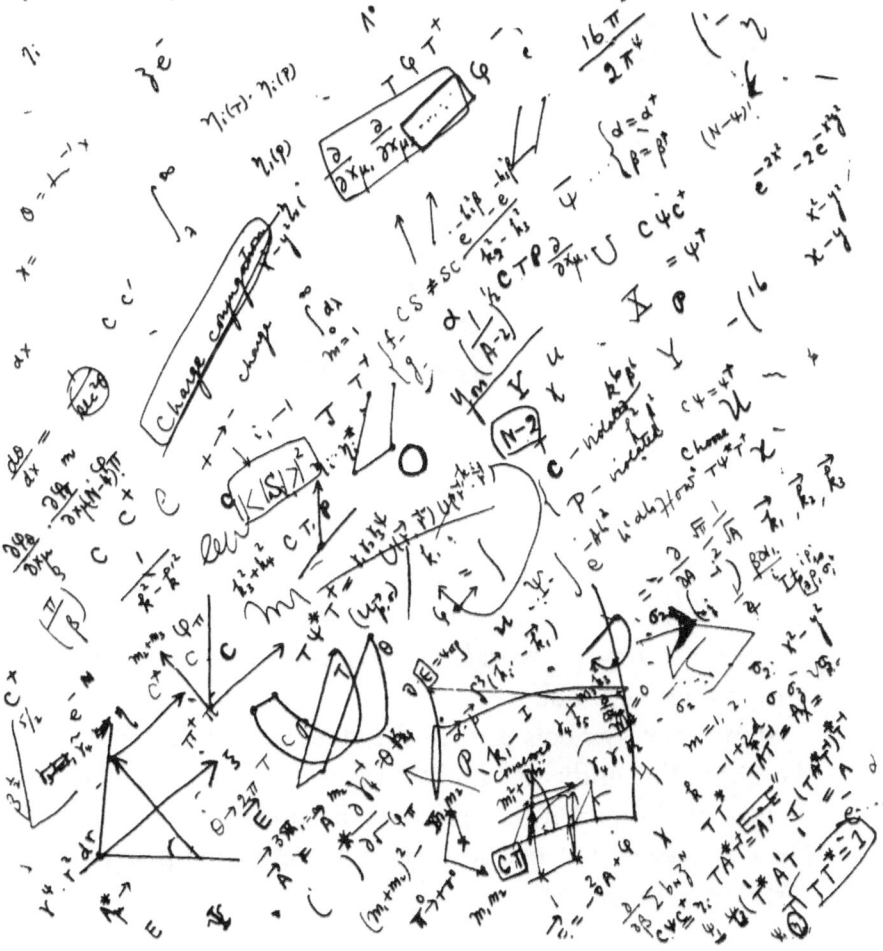

Maps make sense to us in a number of ways. They show us the shape and position of the land and the names of places. We can learn much more from them than that, though, because there are map symbols that identify both natural features and man-made objects. Map symbols are the language of maps. They say much more in a small space than could possibly be said in words.

Long ago, early people drew crude maps to show the part of the world that they explored. They invented their own symbols to show places that were important to them, perhaps a spring that gave fresh water all year round, or the best place to look for berries in season.

In ancient times, little was known about the shape of the world itself and about the continents on it. One early Christian idea of the world was shown by a symbol called the "Orb of the World":

In this diagram the center of the world was Jerusalem, the holy city. The upper half of the circle was Asia. The vertical line in the lower half was the Mediterranean Sea. On its right was Africa; on its left, Europe. Of course this is a symbol for the world, not a map, but it is a kind of geographical symbol.

Many map symbols are used today. One of the oldest is the circle that indicates a city. Early maps showed a small picture of the city itself. Perhaps the present circle-symbol for a city grew out of the fact that the walled-in cities of early times tended to be round.

Map symbols are now fairly well standardized. Many of them are pictographs that look something like the objects they represent. Others are abstract designs. Here are a few map symbols for man-made features:

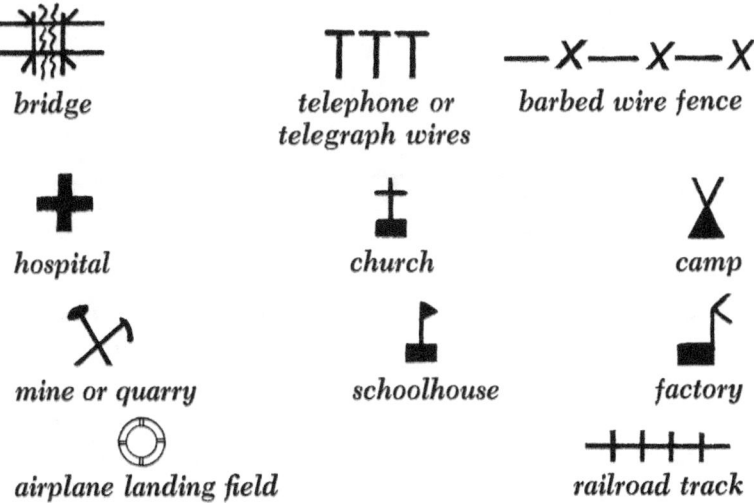

bridge

telephone or
telegraph wires

barbed wire fence

hospital

church

camp

mine or quarry

schoolhouse

factory

airplane landing field

railroad track

Natural features are shown like this:

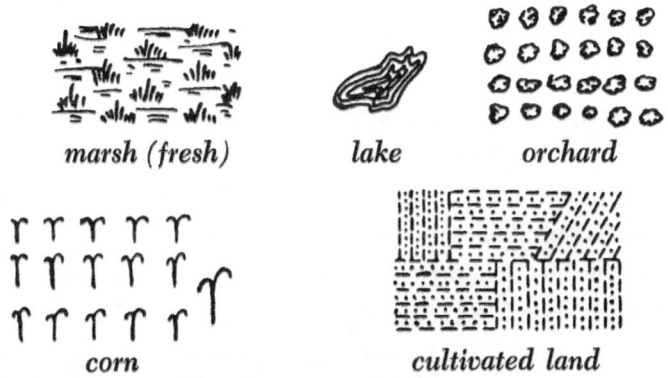

marsh (fresh)

lake

orchard

corn

cultivated land

A "legend" near one edge of a map explains the symbols. Of course, to read the legend on an English-language map you would have to know how to read English. Once the symbols are learned, however, they communicate information to people of any language.

Traveling cattlemen and other people in the early days of our country needed maps that indicated the approximate location of animals on the range. The symbols they used were sometimes taken from Indian pictographs:

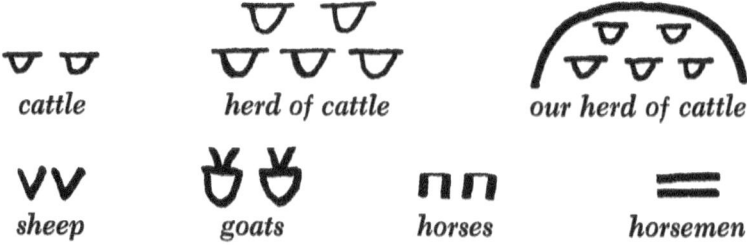

cattle   herd of cattle   our herd of cattle

sheep   goats   horses   horsemen

Often, these maps were hastily sketched by the rangers themselves. But the rangers knew what they needed on a map, and so the rough ones they drew served the purpose.

When architects make plans for a building, they are making a kind of map too. The chief difference is that usually the house does not yet exist. The architect's drawing indicates the arrangement of rooms, the appearance of the building, the materials to be used (such as brick, steel, wood), and many other details. The drawing is a sort of cross-section of the proposed building.

A builder has to know how to read the architect's symbols. He may see the following on a plan for a building, for instance:

The builder knows that this indicates an outside wall with two windows. Numerals on the plan tell him the length of the wall and the width of each window.

The materials to be used for the walls and other parts of a building can be shown like this:

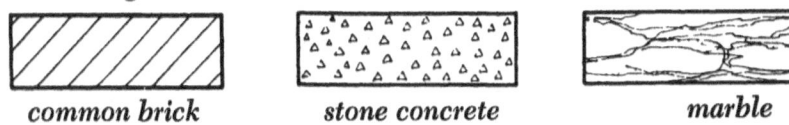

common brick   stone concrete   marble

Instructions for the electrician must be included on the plan too. A double outlet for plugging in lamps and other fixtures is shown this way, right next to the wall where it is to be installed

Here are other symbols for the electrician:

floor outlet   buzzer   bell   telephone

Besides knowing how to read an architect's plan, an electrician must learn a special set of symbols that indicates what kind of electric wiring, switches, or connections are needed on a particular job. Symbols of this kind have been fairly well standardized in this country.

Imagine the confusion that would result if these symbols were *not* generally understood by electricians! An electrician who could not interpret the symbols that are his instructions might put in the wrong kind of switches and connect the wrong wires. Worse than just confusion might result. Wrong electric connections can cause fire.

Here are a few electrician's symbols:

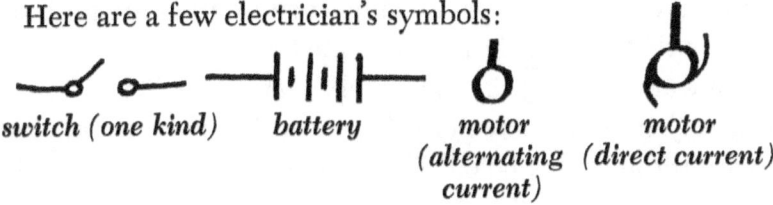

switch (one kind)   battery   motor   motor
                                    (alternating   (direct current)
                                     current)

Plumbers too use special symbols:

thermometer:

valves:

hot-water pipes:

cold-water pipes:

The following interesting patterns are for pipe fittings, to show where pipes cross:

If you were a plumber, all these designs would make sense to you.

A few symbols for radio and television:

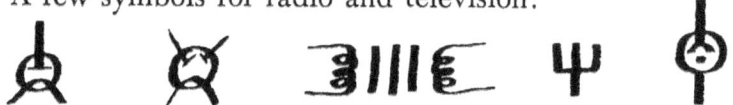

Most of the signs and symbols we have been talking about have a fairly well established meaning and use. This is not true of many signs and symbols used in industry. Here is what can happen: One factory may make a set of symbols for its workers to use in order to get things done efficiently. Another factory may do the same. Without knowing it, the two factories may choose the same symbols and give them quite different meanings. Usually, such symbols are abstract designs that can easily be duplicated.

For example, ▣ in one factory may mean, "Put a screw in here." In another factory the same sign may mean, "Put a wire through this hole." The difference in meaning might not matter if the factory had little connection with the out-side world. But of course a factory makes things *for* the outside world. And the workers live in the outside world. There is a need for symbols that can be understood every-where.

Even more important than the signs and symbols used inside the factory are those used outside. Goods are sent out from factories with shipping instructions and directions for use. All these must be understood by people who speak various languages, in many parts of the world. Signs can help.

Take machines like tractors, harvesters, shoemaking ma-chines, electric generators, and computers. They are made in the United States, Great Britain, France, and Germany, and sent to many other countries. The people who have to operate the machines often cannot read instructions printed in the language of the manufacturer. What can the manu-facturer do about this?

One thing he can do is to have the instructions translated into the language of the man who is to operate the machine. This requires someone who knows both languages well enough to translate clearly. Such people are hard to find. Besides, the operator of the machine may not be able to read at all. But if easily learned signs are put on the control panels of these machines, an operator in India, Chile, New Guinea, or Zambia has little trouble learning what to do.

Signs have been proposed for "start" and "stop," "power on" and "power off," and so on. The International Organiza-tion for Standardization is helping to work out clear, simple industrial signs for use throughout the world. Planning these signs and getting everyone to accept them is a very compli-cated business. Help is needed, not only from engineers and manufacturers, but also from designers who understand how a particular pattern will look to the man or woman who has to use it.

In this country, the United States of America Standards Institute is working at developing signs and symbols for industry. We need an accepted set of symbols for each industry and each occupation that uses symbols. And it is not always *more* symbols that we need. In some fields of industry and engineering there are already too many. Sometimes each separate division of an industry has its own symbols, incomprehensible to everyone else. This can cause the worst kind of confusion. Signs would also be useful outside of industry, on such things as washing machines and dishwashers used in the home.

Deere & Company, a manufacturer of industrial and farm equipment in the United States, has proposed some symbols to help the operators of their machines. These symbols were worked out by industrial designers who carefully studied symbols already in use and kept those that were satisfactory. Others were changed to suit the needs of the operators of the machines. Still others are entirely new.

Here are some of these symbols:

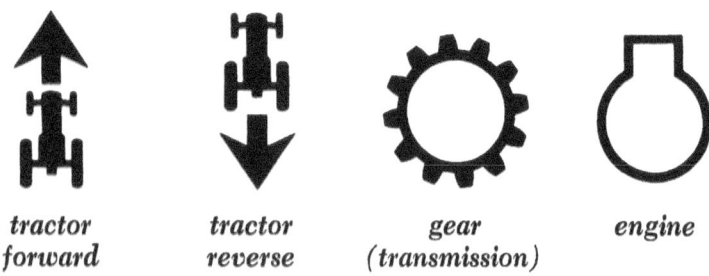

| *tractor forward* | *tractor reverse* | *gear (transmission)* | *engine* |

Notice that the up-and-down symbol shows an abstract object apparently moving *up* and away from something horizontal (the ground, perhaps?) or *down* toward it.

Symbols can be combined:

engine water temperature   *transmission oil temperature*

These symbols are being tried out on the machines made by this company. If necessary, they will be further changed to make them more useful. New ones may be added. If operators of machines all over the world find these symbols practical, they may be adopted by other manufacturers. The happy result may be a standard set of symbols for industrial and farm machines. Certainly such signs are needed.

There is probably no machine more typical of our modern world than the electronic computer. Although it has been called a mechanical brain, it does not think. When certain information is fed into it, a computer can perform mathematical or logical operations with the information. It can then supply the results of these operations in the form of new information. The greatest advantage of a computer is speed. It can solve a million math problems in the time it would take a man to do just one.

Computers can also analyze information about people, the weather, and a variety of scientific matters such as the thrust of a rocket that is going into outer space.

In addition to information, instructions must be fed into a computer to tell it what to do with the information. Both information and instructions are in the form of a "machine language." Each computer has its own machine language, which consists of groups of letters or numbers or other symbols. These are called "machine words."

Most machine languages are very complicated. Many people who need to use computers cannot take the time to learn all the details of the machine language for just one computer, to say nothing of the languages for several computers. You can imagine how difficult it would be if you will think what it is like to switch from one spoken language to another.

Having to learn a machine language could slow up the process of using a computer and even at times prevent its use altogether. For this reason, symbolic languages have been developed for use with computers. These languages are a combination of letters and numerals and sometimes other symbols.

Briefly, this is how a symbolic language is used: The programmer who is preparing to use a computer writes the necessary information in a specific symbolic language, following a given set of rules. The result is called a "source program." The source program then has to be translated into the machine language that the computer can actually use. A special set of instructions in the storage segment of the computer takes care of this. Once the source program has been translated into machine language, it is fed into the computer in the usual way. Machine language can be fed into a computer in the form of a coded scheme, using punched cards or paper tape, magnetic tape, magnetic ink characters, and so on. This is called "input."

When the computer has gone through the required process with the information that was fed into it, it prints the results, one line at a time. This is called "output." Output can be in plain English or in numerals or scientific symbols, punched cards or magnetic tape.

Whatever the form of the results, the whole process starts with the symbolic language. Some of the characters in symbolic languages are familiar symbols such as squares, circles, numerals, and letters. Others are unfamiliar shapes. There is no end to the variety of symbols that can be used. It is limited only by the imagination of the designer of the symbolic language.

The designer tries to select for his symbolic language characters that already have a meaning for the user of the language. When he can do this, the language can be learned much more easily. Sometimes, however, characters are chosen simply because they are convenient, regardless of their previous meaning. In this use they become symbols without a history.

Entirely different symbols in different symbolic languages may refer to the same aspect of the computer program. This can cause trouble for programmers who have to switch from one symbolic language to another. Perhaps in the future an agreement can be worked out so that the same symbols in all the symbolic languages will have the same meaning.

Symbolic languages have a variety of made-up names. FORTRAN is one. This comes from Formula Translation. COBOL means Commercial or Business Orientated Language. COLASL stands for Compiler of the Los Alamos Scientific Laboratory.

COLASL, like all symbolic languages, is designed to simplify communication between the people who must use the computer and the computer itself. In this case, the users of the computer are scientists at Los Alamos Scientific Laboratory in New Mexico. The COLASL symbolic language makes it possible for these scientists to prepare a problem for the computer in a much shorter time than they otherwise could. This is a considerable advantage.

COLASL is written in sentences and even uses punctuation marks. A source program in the COLASL language is typed on a special typewriter and is fed into a computer called STRETCH on input cards. Output is printed in the COLASL alphabet.

The COLASL alphabet includes our own alphabet, *a* through *z*, small letters and capitals, all the numerals, the usual punctuation marks, and many other symbols. Here are some of these:

$$\Delta \quad \partial \quad \cap \quad \cup \quad \infty \quad \nabla \quad \$ \quad \times \quad \div \quad \omega \quad \pi$$

Symbols can be changed by printing a circle or a square around them or various characters above them. Thus:

a a̲ # e e⃝ ω ω⃖ z z⃝ z⃞ z⃟

Computers are manufactured in just a few countries, but they are sold to many others. A sign system has been proposed by designers for one manufacturer to help people who speak different languages with the operation of these machines. These signs would appear on the console of the computer, for the use of the operator. Here are two:

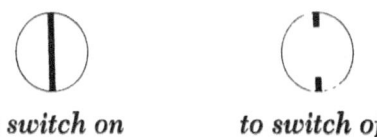

to switch on   *to switch off*

If there is an error, this sign will light up on the console of the computer:

stop! mistake!

Some of the signs can be combined to create new meanings.

This whole system of signs had to be designed without reference to any earlier ones, since there were no signs of any kind for computers. The designers also had to allow for many changes because computers themselves are changing so rapidly.

The meaning of these signs has to be learned. But, as we have seen, this is easier than learning an unfamiliar language. Notice the simplicity of the designs. They are easy to remember.

The whole field of signs and symbols in science and industry constantly grows broader and more complex. Although it is touched on only briefly here, the need for such symbols, and for careful planning and good design in creating them, is of major importance today.

8 /

Trails
and
Journeys

Have you ever used trail signs on a hike? You may have placed sticks or stones in patterns that meant "This is the way," or "Turn right." Long grasses can be tied in bunches to convey the same message to those who are following your trail.

Trail signs are sometimes chalked on buildings or on trees. They can also be scratched into the ground with a pointed stick. Here are some Boy Scout trail signs:

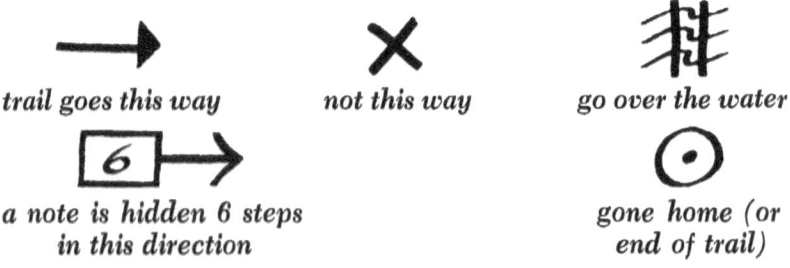

trail goes this way   not this way   go over the water

a note is hidden 6 steps
in this direction

gone home (or
end of trail)

The last sign shows a person in a tent. It is also the ancient Egyptian and Chinese sign for "sun," and the American Indian sign for "spirit," which shows us, again, what different meanings the same sign can have for different people.

Explorers and other travelers in our western wilderness needed signs on the trail, too. Some of theirs were adapted from Indian trail signs. Here are a few:

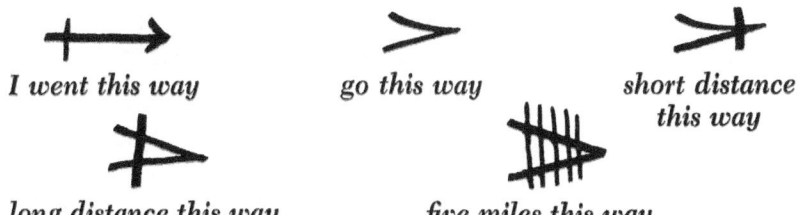

I went this way   *go this way*   *short distance this way*

long distance this way   *five miles this way*

Probably the people who have traveled the longest distances on foot are hoboes and gypsies. These people have highly practical graphic signs for communicating with one another. The true hobo is not a thief. Nor does he consider himself a tramp. He says he simply prefers to see the world without spending money and without doing any work if he can avoid it. He is constantly on the move. Though he usually travels alone, he considers himself a member of the once-sizable group that travels as he does. Hoboes call themselves "Knights of the Road." They have even published a newspaper under that title.

All hoboes have the daily problem of finding food and shelter along the road. Each one takes seriously the responsibility of leaving behind him, in each town he visits, signs that will communicate the local situation to the next hobo who comes along.

Take a fictional hobo, Joe Busby. Joe jumped off a freight train in a small town and began to look around. On a fence near the railroad, he saw a sign drawn with chalk:

Joe recognized this as a closed eye, meaning that the town was asleep—that is, the police were not looking for hoboes.

So he decided to stay. Farther along the fence, this sign told him to take the next street on his right:

He started off. The day was hot, and Joe was getting discouraged, when he saw a sign on a tree:

He knew this meant "Don't give up! Never say die!" So he plodded on.

Soon, on a green picket fence surrounding a large white house, he found this sign:

This meant that a kindhearted woman lived there. Farther along on the same fence he saw:

To Joe Busby this said, "Tell a pitiful story." (The three small triangles probably once represented children.) Joe rang the doorbell of the white house, told a sad story to the kindhearted woman, and was rewarded with two peanut-butter sandwiches and a glass of milk.

Later, as he continued down the street, a fierce dog rushed out of a house and nipped his leg. Joe drew a sign on the telephone pole near the house:

 *(A comb has sharp teeth. So does a dog.)*

The next hobo who came along would know Joe's message meant "Bad dog here."

At another town, a hobo named Sam Haskins arrived on

foot. On the outskirts of town he found a sign on a telephone pole:

This meant "Open eye, police are looking for hoboes." It was bad news for Sam, who was tired and hungry.

There was a farmhouse nearby and Sam approached it, hoping that he could at least get a sandwich. He was stopped by a sign chalked on a tree in the driveway:

Sam knew this meant "Man with gun." Wearily he turned back to the road and prepared to hitch a ride away from town.

Here are more hobo signs:

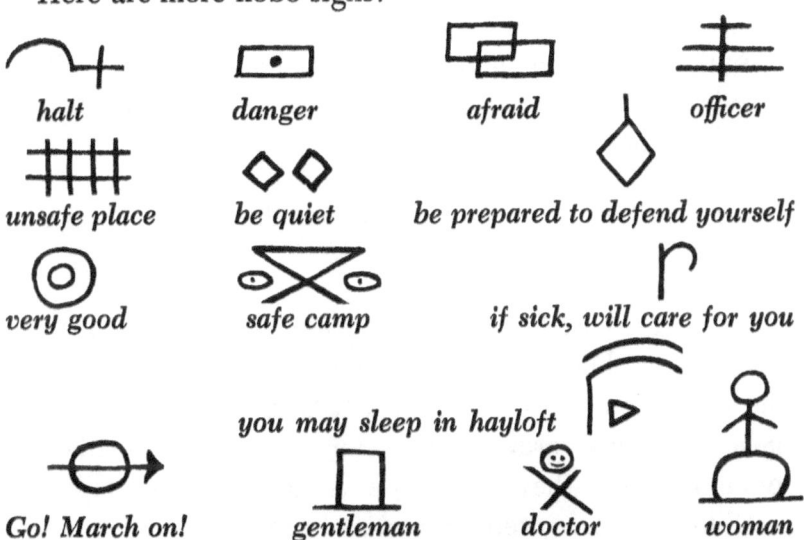

Here is a sign made by European hoboes and gypsies:

This conveys quite a message: "Two children [zeroes!], four men, and three women passed this way."

Hobo signs have a long history. They have been traced back to wandering gangs in Europe during the Middle Ages. Gypsies also used them. In England, peddlers who sold household goods and trinkets around the countryside adapted the signs for their own purposes. For example, to them ⌒‿ meant "Keep going. I have called here and it's no go." ⌒⤳✝ meant "Stop. This is a good place to try selling."

Tradesmen in towns had their own signs. Both of the following meant "Careful! Watch out for thieves!"

Some of these signs have an even longer history. They were borrowed by vagabonds from ancient books of magic. The "halt" or "stop" sign is one of these: ⌒⤳✝

Here is another: 𝄞⤳ To hoboes this means, "You can get food here by working."

All the signs used by hoboes, gypsies, and other wanderers grew out of their need to communicate with one another. The signs were not created by artists, designers, or technicians. They just grew. But because they were made for communication, they had to be as clear and as simple as possible. The signs were drawn, and drawn again, by imaginative and ingenious wanderers, and in the process they acquired the elements of good design.

Hobo signs have lost most of their secrecy. In any case, there are now few hoboes and gypsies on the road. They do not seem to fit in with the modern age of the machine. Their signs remain to intrigue us, though. You might find some of them useful yourself, but don't start chalking up all the fences and telephone poles in your neighborhood! Remember that the true wanderer works very quietly and secretly. He makes his mark just here and there, where most of the people who pass by will not even notice it.

On the pavement at a nearby street corner, you might one day find chalked signs like these:

These are instructions for the men who distribute free samples and similar things from door to door.

Hobo signs are unofficial road signs. There are many others. Some date back to early times. Here is an early American Indian sign carved on the rock near a steep trail in New Mexico:

This sign warns of danger. It says that a goat could climb up the rocky trail, but if a horse tried it he would surely tumble down. Other rock carvings in our southwestern states were probably also made for the guidance of travelers.

One American Indian sign warns the traveler to go no farther. He will be shot for trespassing.

The highways in ancient times needed very few signs. There were not many travelers and they had little choice of roads. And, since it was impossible to go very fast, most of the dangers along the road could be sighted well in advance.

One of the earliest road signs was the "fingerboard," shaped like a long hand with a pointing finger. It showed the way to the next town. Later, an arrow was used for the same purpose: ⬅ Chesham 5

Today, all over the world, there are millions of automobiles on the road, and most of the drivers are in a hurry to get somewhere. People travel not only in their own countries but in other countries, on other continents, sometimes half a world away.

All this traveling has created any number of problems. People have to know which side of the road to drive on, where to go, when to stop, how to be careful. Signs were designed, often hastily, to communicate this information.

In Europe, each country put up its own signs. In this country, each state could at first do as it pleased about them. Many of the early signs relied heavily on words, always in the language of the country that put them up. In parts of Canada, both French and English were used. Because a majority of the people speak English in the United States, signs in English work out well for most of those who live here. It is not so easy for people from other countries who come here to visit, or for Americans who, for example, speak Spanish instead of English.

About sixty different languages are spoken in Europe. Road signs using the language spoken by local people often meant nothing at all to everyone else. Imagine trying to drive a car on a modern highway without knowing what the road signs mean! It would be almost impossible, certainly dangerous.

The solution to the problem has been to set up signs without words that can be accepted and understood by people of different countries, whatever their language. These graphic signs are, in any case, more efficient than signs with words. People can "read" them faster.

All the standard road signs have had to be specially designed, since there were none available from earlier times. Designing signs for general use was not as easy as you might think. People like their own way of doing things. Often they are more eager to have other people do things *their* way than to make any changes themselves.

Automobile clubs in Europe did try to design a few standard signs in the early part of this century. Here are two proposed by a Swiss automobile magazine in 1923:

(Does a snail mean "slow" to you? Or "slimy"?) These signs were never adopted for international use.

The situation remained quite confused until the United Nations held a Conference on Road and Motor Transport in 1949. A committee of experts was appointed to design a set of practical signs for international use. There are now more than sixty of these international signs for regulating traffic, and only two of them use words at all. These signs are not all new. Some are based on earlier signs that were used in various countries.

The international road signs have three basic shapes:

warning,	*signs giving orders*	*for information,*
for danger	*or instructions*	*such as location*
		of telephone

Inside these shapes, some signs have pictographs, designs that look like the object they are telling about, such as a telephone or a bicycle. Others are abstract. The best-known abstract design, used everywhere, is the arrow.

The international road signs have been adopted by more than thirty countries, most of them in Europe, but some in Southeast Asia, Africa, and South America. Great Britain changed to the international signs just recently, adopting most of them and adding others. The added ones were designed within the basic international shapes.

The most important thing for a driver to know is when to stop. Here is the international STOP sign:

This sign is always red. Once anyone learns it, no matter what his language is, he will know at least one English word, STOP. This will be useful to a foreign motorist in the United States, for the international road signs are not used here.

Our road signs were fairly well established before the in-

ternational road signs were introduced. At first, our signs
were quite different in different parts of the country. Recently, however, there has been an attempt to standardize
them. It was decided not to change to the international signs,
even though ours depend to a considerable extent on English
words.

Our STOP sign looks like this: **STOP**

The standard color for a STOP sign in this country is now
red. Some, however, are yellow and some are brown. But,
unmistakably, the sign says STOP.

If a foreign motorist cannot read any English words other
than "stop," he will have trouble with many of the road signs
in the United States. They rely heavily on words. What will
he do when he sees signs that read "Do Not Pass," "Road
Closed," or "Speed Zone"?

To be sure, some of our signs do not use words. This one
is fairly clear:

But it, too, differs in both color and shape from the international sign for curve. (Ours is yellow, theirs red.)

Here are other international signs:
Warnings:

dangerous curve

slippery road

quay or riverbank

Instructions:

*do not enter
(red)*

*no horn-blowing
(black on red)*

*bicycles must use
THIS path (blue)*

Information:

*camping site
(black on blue)*

*youth hostel
(black on blue)*

*filling station
(black on blue)*

Of course, very few signs are so clear in their meaning that everyone can understand them at a glance. People's minds do not all work the same way. The international road signs have been made as clear and as simple as possible. But a motorist driving through a country that uses these signs should learn them in advance. He can get a folder that shows pictures of the signs and gives an explanation of them in his own language. Learning the meaning of the signs is much easier, though, than learning a new language.

The international road sign system is a useful means of communication for our modern world. More and more countries are adopting it. However, even within the limits of the basic designs, there is still room for refreshing differences. Here are some of these, not all from countries using the international system:

Pedestrian crossing signs:

International   *Great Britain (no hat!)*   *Southern Rhodesia*

Australia

Japan

Saudi Arabia

The pedestrian on the international sign, and on others, wears European clothes. Is this really international? In many parts of the world men do not dress this way. Perhaps a more abstract sign would be better.

There is a good reason why the figure on the Saudi Arabian sign is headless. Followers of the Moslem religion do not approve of any form of human image. But they will accept a traffic sign that shows a *headless* person.

Path for pedestrians, all sizes (international sign):

Animals crossing:

International

Great Britain, wild animals

Great Britain, horses or ponies

Southern Rhodesia, elephant crossing   *Kenya, cattle crossing*

School crossing or "children crossing" signs are quite different in different places. The international sign shows two children, of different sizes, walking along. On the British sign they are in a hurry; they run. The school crossing sign in Denmark shows an earnest little girl with pigtail flying, leading her reluctant brother. Israel's children walk sedately. In India, a boy runs along quite gaily.

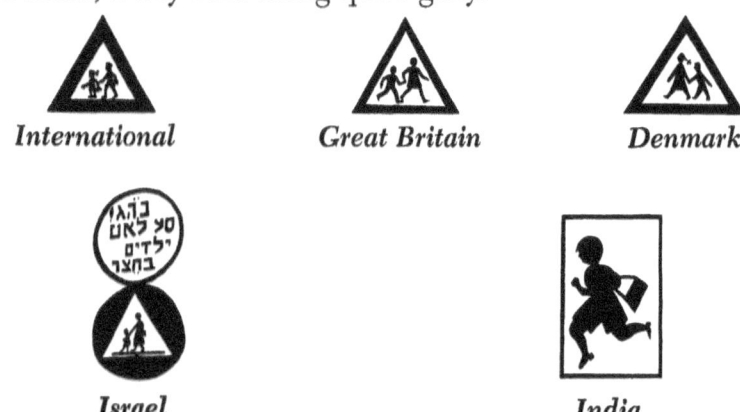

International · Great Britain · Denmark

Israel · India

Road signs are a kind of international language, cutting across language barriers. You might also call them communication for safety. The purpose of most such signs is to make sure that motorists drive carefully so that no one will get hurt.

No country today *has* to use the signs proposed by the United Nations committee in 1949. But the United Nations itself is the greatest force for international cooperation in the world. All the member countries know that the road signs created and recommended by a committee of the United Nations are designed for use anywhere in the world. As a result, the organizations that regulate traffic in each country take the international road signs seriously. The signs have become an important influence toward understanding among people all over the world.

9 /

Sign
Writing
for
Today

In early times, there was no need for an international language. Few people traveled far from home. Few encountered anyone who spoke a language different from their own. Later, as we have seen, merchants who traveled to other countries, buying and selling goods, invented numerals that all of them could use, whatever their language. They carried alphabets and writing from one country to another. But spoken words were always more important than written ones, and languages kept their own special characteristics in different places.

Today, more than ever before, we need some sort of international language. More and more people travel, and some go to live in faraway places for long periods of time. All over the world people must communicate with other people who speak different languages. If they can neither talk together nor read the same things, there is little understanding between them. Most people cannot learn more than a few languages. Many never have a chance to learn any language but their own.

The idea of creating a single spoken and written language for international use has intrigued people for many years. There have been more than 200 attempts to invent such a language. One of these is called Esperanto. A description of it was first published under the pen name Dr. Esperanto, which means Dr. Hopeful. Esperanto uses most of the letters of our alphabet and basic words from the leading languages of Europe. There are magazines published in Esperanto, textbooks printed in more than seventy languages, and thousands of other books. Thousands of teachers are qualified to teach Esperanto.

Nevertheless, neither Esperanto nor any other invented language has been adopted for general use. All of them are artificial languages, and they remain foreign to all nations. Perhaps an international language would seem less artificial if it were taught to children in the earliest grades. Then they might grow up taking it for granted.

Basic English is another attempt at an international language. Since millions of people speak English, Basic English is not "invented." It is part of a language that is already in wide use. In our country, Basic English is used to teach English to adult foreigners, so that they can adjust as quickly as possible to our way of life.

Basic English uses 850 English words. Altogether, the English language has hundreds of thousands of words, but most people use only a few thousand. The words chosen for Basic English are just the most necessary ones.

Pictures are often used in teaching Basic English. For example, a picture of fish in an aquarium shows "up," "down," "under," "over," according to where the fish are or which way they are going. The words are printed beside the fish.

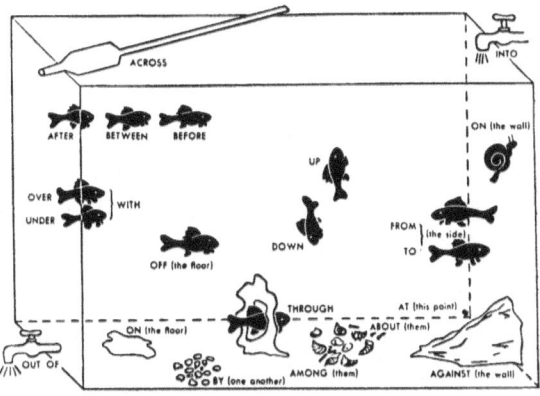

In spite of all these attempts at international languages, the fact is that signs and symbols can get some meanings across better and quicker than words. One of the principal tasks in international communication at present is to develop pictographs and other signs that can convey a simple meaning to everyone, at a glance.

We have seen what the designers of road signs did about this problem. Their signs had the advantage of being promoted by an international organization, the United Nations. Any written signs developed today are sure to be severely limited in their use unless they are accepted by people in many parts of the world. Representatives of international organizations, or nations, must get together and agree on the kind of pictographs and other signs that are to be used.

One useful system of picture writing is called ISOTYPE. This was developed by Dr. Otto Neurath, in Vienna, Austria.

The word ISOTYPE is an abbreviation for International System of Typographic Picture Education. ISOTYPE pictographs were not intended to take the place of language. They were to be used along with language, to make certain ideas clearer than they would be with words alone.

The main use of ISOTYPE is for education, though it has had other uses, too. Each ISOTYPE pictograph is a simplified picture of the object it stands for. In this respect, ISOTYPE has something in common with earlier picture signs. The difference is that ISOTYPE is specially designed, and so its meaning is often clearer than, for instance, Indian picture writing or Egyptian hieroglyphs. There are little ISOTYPE men, women and children, cows, cars, ships and sheep. A single glance at one of these figures is supposed to reveal the most important features of the object represented. There are no unnecessary details.

Here are a few ISOTYPE figures:

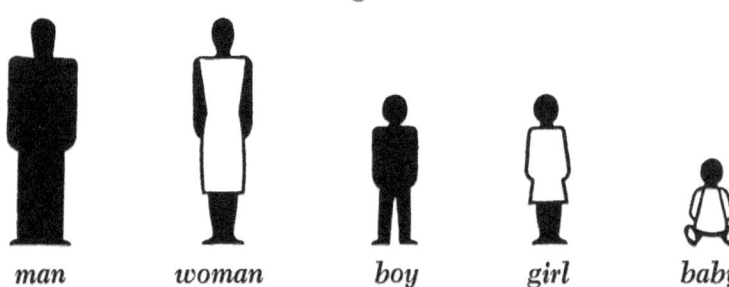

man   *woman*   *boy*   *girl*   *baby*

Dr. Neurath thought of his pictographs as forming the basis for an international picture language. It was his aim to establish contacts with other countries, to further the adoption of ISOTYPE. Although the system was not universally accepted, ISOTYPE symbols have been widely used ever since in Europe and in this country.

The Isotype Institute in England developed diagrams for children's books, to show such geographical features as mountains, streams, glaciers, and deserts. These, too, are simplified pictures of the things they represent. You might not learn a great deal of geography from the diagrams alone, but along with the words in the text, they give a vivid impression of land and water and their uses. Other diagrams show man at work on the land and on the water.

The ISOTYPE system of signs has had great influence on the figures used in graphs—that is, the diagrams showing such facts as the numbers of people or things existing at different times or in different places. Graphs make this information clearer and easier to understand than it would be in words only.

Here are samples of one kind of graph. These are diagrams showing how much land of different types there was in the United States at different times. The land is identified by a simplified drawing of the principal thing growing on it. These are pictographs, much like ISOTYPE. Pictographs of this kind are often called symbols. (Each symbol in the graphs below represents 100 million acres.)

Cropland:

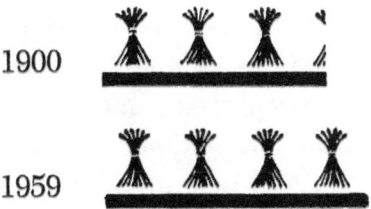

1900

1959

Grassland:

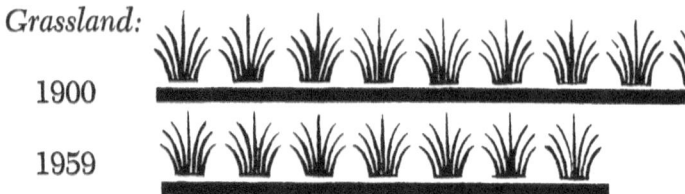

1900

1959

Forest and woodland:

1900

1959

There have been a number of attempts to create a complete world writing system with signs. This is not the same thing as an international language, which can be spoken as well as written.

About 300 years ago, in the seventeenth century, an Englishman named John Wilkins invented a system of universal characters. These characters were abstract; they were not made to look like the things they represented or, in fact, like any real object at all. Some of the characters looked very much like each other, with the result that they were hard to learn. Wilkins' system was much too complicated for general application, and no one uses it now.

The famous mathematician and philosopher Leibnitz, who also lived in the seventeenth century, thought a great deal about the need for a universal system of written signs. He was fascinated by the sign writing of the Chinese, but thought that something much simpler and more practical would have to be developed for international use. He did not think Wilkins' system would do. Leibnitz himself, however, never found the time to work out his own system.

Others have tried. Symbols for world writing have recently been devised by an Australian, C.K. Bliss. He calls his system "Semantography," a made-up word that means "writing for meaning."

Semantography is a workable system, once it is learned. It does not depend on the sounds of spoken words, and for this reason it can be used by people everywhere, whatever their language. Most of the symbols in Semantography are made up of lines that follow the outlines of real things. This makes them easier to learn than symbols that do not look like anything at all. Specific things are represented by simplified pictographs. There is ⋏ for "tree," ◯ for "sun."

Ideas are harder to relate to real things, but this problem has been worked out, too. Semantography is more than just picture writing. Almost anything that can be written can be translated into Semantography, though it would be difficult to translate complicated ideas precisely. This is difficult in our everyday language, too.

Semantography can be read in all languages. If you speak English, for instance, you would translate Semantography into English as you read, putting the words into the order you are familiar with. If you speak French, you would translate Semantography into that language, arranging the words as they are normally spoken in French. And so on.

The lines that make up each symbol are simple straight lines and curves, with the same lines repeated in different arrangements. They can, in fact, be typed on a specially adapted typewriter. For general use, the symbols would be the same size as regular print. Here, to show them more clearly, they are somewhat larger.

Semantography is not meant to take the place of any real

language. It cannot be spoken. In any case, no one would want to give up speaking and writing the comfortable language he was brought up with. Besides, the languages we speak have more meaning than any invented language, spoken or written. They are composed of words that have lived and changed for thousands of years as people used them.

The greatest advantage of a symbol writing like Semantography is that it can be written and read by people who speak different languages. It can make communication possible across the world.

If you were to use Semantography as a real tool for writing, you would have to practice writing the symbols until you could remember them and write them easily. This is not as hard as you might think because the symbols make so much sense.

You already know some of the symbols. Semantography uses the numerals and mathematical signs $+ - \times :$ (for "divide") and $=$. (These and a few others are the only symbols in Semantography that are not related to real things.)

Here are some other symbols you might learn at the beginning:

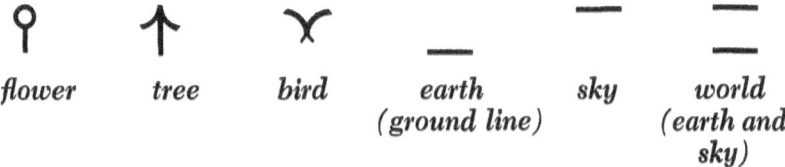

| flower | tree | bird | earth (ground line) | sky | world (earth and sky) |

These are all *things*. But things are sometimes active; they move. How can sign writing indicate action? Semantogra-

phy does it by placing an action sign above a symbol: ∧
(This sign suggests pushing up, as the cone of a volcano
pushes up, a sort of "growing" action.)

Let's see how this works. Here is Semantography for "legs
and feet":
∧

And here is Semantography for action with your legs—"to
walk," "to go," and so on:
∧
∧

(The ancient Egyptians used this sign for "legs." When they
wanted to indicate "walking," they used the same sign,
meaning the *idea* of moving with your legs.)

Here is more Semantography:

⊙   ∧
                                     ⊙
eye   *to see, etc.*

(We have seen this eye symbol before. It was the Egyptian
symbol for "sun.")

Now let's combine some of these signs:

Bird   *sees*   *flower*   *and*   *tree.*

There is not space here for a full lesson in the writing of
Semantography. But we can look at a few more samples, to
see how the symbols are worked out.

Signs for "coming" and "going":

⊓   ⊬⊓   ⌐+

door   *entrance*   *exit*

The last two of these could be used in public buildings.

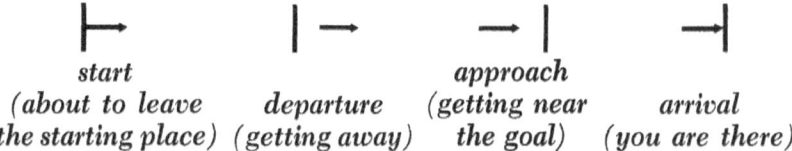

start
(about to leave the starting place)   *departure (getting away)*   *approach (getting near the goal)*   *arrival (you are there)*

The meaning is conveyed by the position of the arrow with relation to a straight line.

Signs about feelings:

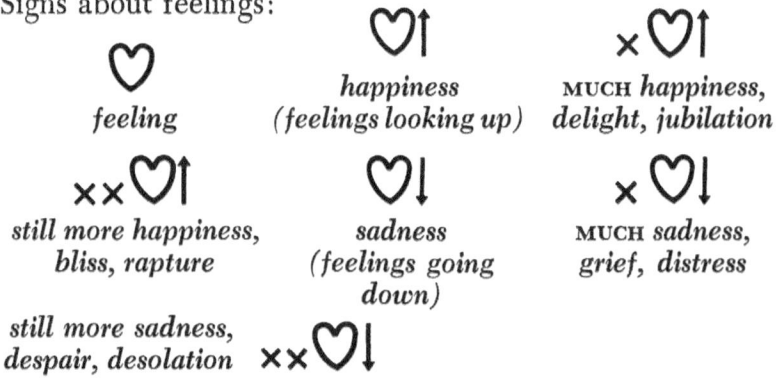

feeling

happiness (feelings looking up)

MUCH *happiness, delight, jubilation*

still more happiness, bliss, rapture

sadness (feelings going down)

MUCH *sadness, grief, distress*

still more sadness, despair, desolation

The X used next to any sign is the same as the multiplication sign in mathematics. In Semantography it means "much" or "many." Here is another example to show how this works:

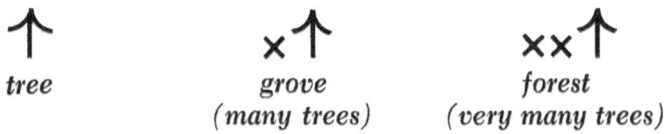

tree

grove (many trees)

forest (very many trees)

Of course, any sign system that intends to cover all of a language must offer more than symbols for people, things, thoughts, and feelings. Here is how Semantography shows time:

past

present

future

These signs represent curved mirrors. The first reflects what we have just written (in the past). The last reflects what we are about to write (in the future). The sign in the center represents the present, a fleeting moment between past and future.

These signs show where things are:

·|	|·	‾·	—
before, *in front of*	*behind,* *after*	*above,* *over*	*below,* *under*

Notice how simple this is. Each meaning is shown by the position of a dot with relation to a straight line.

Symbols for familiar things around us use a variety of combinations:

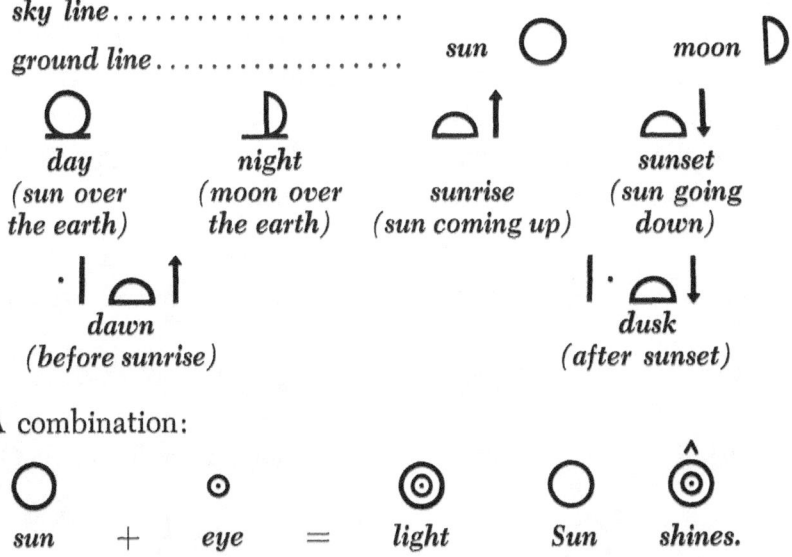

sky line....................

ground line.................

sun ◯   *moon* D

◯	⅁	⌒↑	⌒↓
day *(sun over* *the earth)*	*night* *(moon over* *the earth)*	*sunrise* *(sun coming up)*	*sunset* *(sun going* *down)*

·|⌒↑	|·⌒↓
dawn *(before sunrise)*	*dusk* *(after sunset)*

A combination:

◯	+	⊙	=	◎	◯	◎̂
sun		**eye**		**light**	**Sun**	**shines.**

More familiar things:

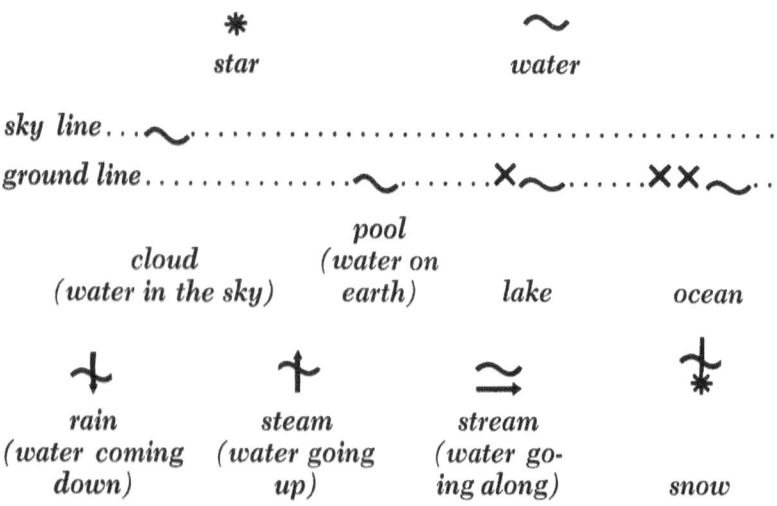

According to Mr. Bliss, many of his symbols are taken from the drawings of children. Others are similar to the symbols used in the picture writings of early man. These are symbols that are likely to seem natural to everyone.

People are not neglected in Semantography. Here are signs for the family of man. The sign for "roof" means much more than that. It means "home." Its outline suggests the outstretched arms of a father and mother.

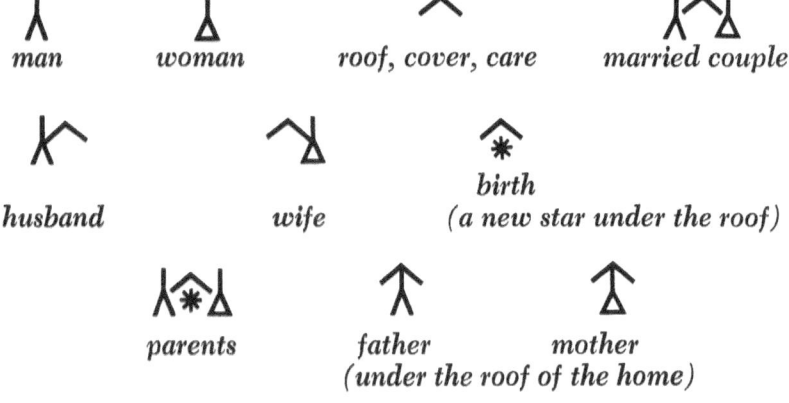

life

This last symbol is a combination of the two symbols for "individual" and "sun": ⊥ ◯

A few simple sentences:

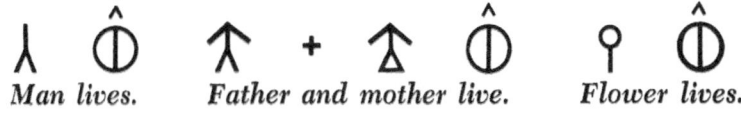

Man lives.   Father and mother live.   Flower lives.

(Notice the little action mark again.)

Just for fun, let's compare some of these family of man symbols with a few from the Middle Ages. These, of course, developed over a longer period of time than Semantography symbols, and they were not planned as part of an international system of sign writing. Instead, they were worked into paintings and carved in the stone of great buildings.

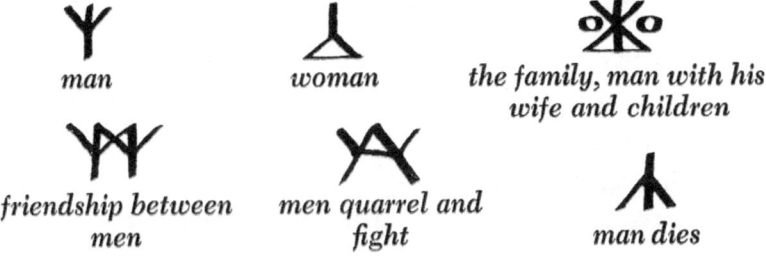

man   woman   the family, man with his
                                          wife and children

friendship between   men quarrel and
men   fight   man dies

If you will look back to the American Indian pictographs, you will see that some of them are similar to the Semantography symbols, too.

Let's try a somewhat longer sentence, using Semantography:

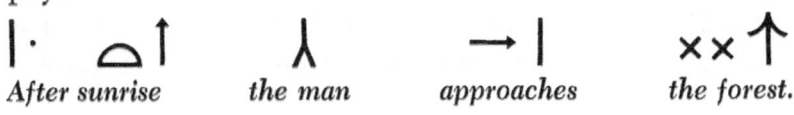

After sunrise   the man   approaches   the forest.

You can write poetry in Semantography, too. Like this:

D	↑	÷	∿∿	∿
Moon	*goes up*	*over*	*waves*	*of water.*

This is easy to read if you know a little Semantography. But try it in Rumanian: *Luna merge in sus deasupra valurile apei.*

See what arrows can do:

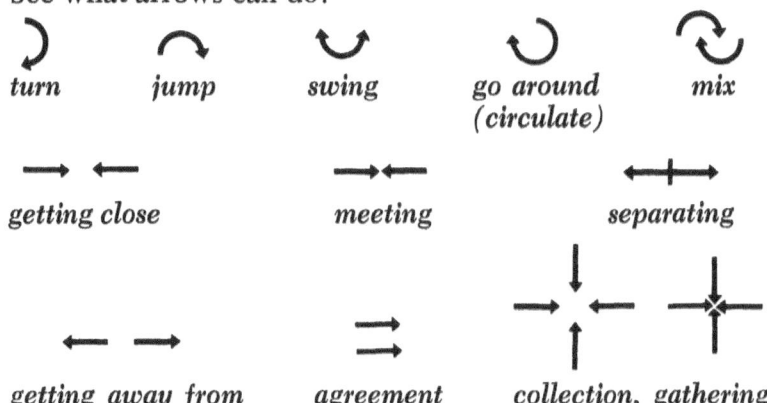

ว	⌒	⌣	↻	↻
turn	*jump*	*swing*	*go around (circulate)*	*mix*

→ ←	→•←	←┼→
getting close	*meeting*	*separating*

← →	⇉	
getting away from	*agreement*	*collection, gathering*

The last two of these symbols can also be used separately, and in that case each has a somewhat different meaning. The first then indicates a gathering in full swing; the second, a gathering that has just ended.

Suppose you could write letters to people anywhere in the world by using a universal symbol writing. You could have friends at the far corners of the earth without having to learn any spoken language other than your own. People everywhere might understand one another as never before. This, Mr. Bliss believes, could truly become "one writing for one world." Whether Semantography will be adopted for international use, we do not know. In any case, Mr. Bliss has made an important contribution to the making of graphic symbols.

You, too, can invent a set of written signs. Start with some of the Semantography signs, if you wish. Then make signs for the things that are important to you. Try them on your friends. Unlike a secret code, your sign writing should be as easy to understand as possible. Its purpose is to get ideas across, not to hide them. Making understandable signs may prove to be more difficult than you think. Of course, not all your signs will be so clear that other people can "read" them without first being told their meaning.

Yours will not be international sign writing. It will be just for fun. No one knows, in fact, just when any system of written signs will be accepted for use throughout the world. It may take a long time.

10/

Signs
and
Symbols
for
Tomorrow

How do we know which signs will be most effective for international use? No one can know until they have been tried out, over and over again. Designing these signs is a job that requires imagination and patience, and a willingness to change.

Abstract signs are in some ways the best. They can mean the same thing to people with very different ways of living, and they seldom get out of date. They may be hard to learn unless the designs have something to do with natural shapes. Once they have been accepted, however, their meaning usually sticks. This is certainly true of such signs as $+$, $-$, ?, 6.

Of course there are some difficulties. An apparently neutral shape can suggest entirely different things to different people. Here is an example. What does this shape mean to you? 0

When a group of people were asked this question, they suggested all sorts of things: a flame, a bag, a pear, a carrot, a parsnip, a knothole, a dog's ear, and so on. A few lines added to the design could make it look like any one of these things.

The same shape in another position suggested still other things:

| mouse | fish | bird | whale | bug | sweet potato |

Imagination adds the details that give this design meaning. Any shape that suggests such varied possibilities probably would not make a good sign for international use.

Pictographs are less easily confused, but they can be used in a confusing way. For example, here is a sign that looks like a pictograph, but it is not used as one. This sign is supposed to mean "fragile." It has often been put on crates of breakable items that are shipped from place to place.

A label bearing this sign was stuck on the top of a small crate of fine glassware that was being shipped to India. When the crate arrived, the dock worker took a look at the label and frowned. The sign did not mean "fragile" to him. It meant just what it looked like: a broken glass. The crate must be full of broken glass! The dock worker could not imagine why anyone would want *that*. But he picked the crate up and threw it onto the back of a truck. It landed with a crash.

We need an international sign, understood everywhere, meaning "fragile." Or perhaps what we need is a series of signs that will show how a breakable package *should* be picked up and put down.

Another example of this kind of misunderstanding is the story of an American who went into a restaurant in Paris on a rainy day. He wanted some mushrooms. He spoke no French; the waiter spoke no English. The American tried drawing a picture of a mushroom on the menu. The waiter brought him an umbrella!

Whether it is a pictograph or an abstract design, a sign is useless unless its meaning is clear—after it has been learned, if not before.

A sign may have a generally accepted meaning and still be unacceptable to certain people for other reasons. To us, a red cross seems a good sign for "First Aid." Surely this would be understood anywhere! It has been adopted as one of the International Road Signs. But to people in Mohammedan countries, such as Turkey, a cross of any kind looks like a Christian symbol. They do not want to use a sign that belongs to another religion. A red crescent suits them better. In fact, a red crescent is used on highways in Turkey and other Mohammedan countries to indicate a First Aid station. Its use in these countries has been approved by the United Nations.

First Aid station
(international road sign)

First Aid station
(road sign in Mohammedan
countries)

There are many other reasons why a sign may be understood in some countries and make no sense to people from other countries. For example, the curled trumpet has been used in some European countries to indicate a post office:

To people in these countries this sign is clear; it always means "post office." But to people in other parts of the world it has no such meaning.

Suppose we were looking for a sign that could be used to indicate a post office anywhere in the world. Such a sign would be very useful to people traveling in a country whose language they did not understand. The Europeans who use the trumpet sign might suggest it as an international sign. They are used to it. But people in other countries have signs of their own for "post office." They are not likely to want to change them. A completely new sign might solve the problem, but only if most countries agreed to use it. You can see how complicated it can be to develop acceptable new signs!

Of course, the meaning of a sign can change or get out of date. This is more likely to happen to pictographs than to abstract signs. The International Road Sign for "railroad crossing," for example, shows a definitely old-fashioned train, quite unlike the streamlined ones of today:

Most people would probably know what this sign represents, but to Americans it might suggest a museum for old trains.

The meaning of abstract signs changes less often than that of pictographs, but it too can change. A good example is the swastika:

This was a symbol known to people in many parts of the world in very early times. As we have seen, people who worshiped the sun as the source of life used this symbol. To people in the Far East, and to Indians in Central and North America, the swastika meant good luck and wisdom. It has often been thought of as a variation of the cross.

It seemed unlikely that the meaning of the swastika would ever change. But it did. The Nazis in Germany chose the swastika for their symbol. When the dictator Hitler took over the government of Germany, the Nazi flag, with a swastika in its center, flew on flagpoles all over the country. The swastika on the flag was turned sideways in a white circle on a red background:

Hitler and his government caused untold suffering to millions of people both inside Germany and elsewhere. Under this flag, German soldiers marched west and east in World

War II. It will be a long time before most Americans and Europeans can think of the swastika as anything but a symbol of war and cruelty.

Some signs must be read almost instantly. Suppose a fire breaks out in a public building, and you have to find a way out at once. In this country you will look for a lighted sign saying EXIT. You do not need to think twice about it. A Frenchman need not think twice about a sign that reads SORTIE, which means "exit" to him.

Neither of these signs would do for use all over the world. Even the letters on the signs are unfamiliar to people in many countries. Designers have been working on signs for "exit" that can be understood everywhere, instantly. Here is one possibility:

Better, perhaps, is the sign for "exit" in Semantography:

Our shelter sign is a good example of an abstract sign that can be understood at a glance:

This sign has been placed on many public buildings and apartment houses in this country. It tells us where to go in case of an air raid or bombing. The sign includes, at the bottom, the words FALLOUT SHELTER, but you can read the triangles on the sign from a distance long before you can read the words.

The designer of signs has to know his job. He must choose the few details that will get a single idea across, and out of these he must make a good design. Too many details, or the wrong ones, can cause confusion. Details that do not make an immediate impression on the viewer may be lost in the "noise" of nearby signs and colors.

A sign should communicate its message so surely that, once learned, it never suggests any other meaning. This is easiest to do when the design is related to the information it is to convey (for example, Semantography for "water": ∿). But it is not always possible to relate the design to the information. Sometimes an entirely abstract design seems the best solution.

A designer knows that straight vertical lines suggest strength and purpose. Horizontal lines suggest quietness. Diagonal lines, on the other hand, give an impression of motion. A dark shape on a light background seems smaller than a light shape on a dark background.

All this, and more, the designer must know and use in his work. The simplest design communicates the best. Signs that have grown naturally through many years of use have often achieved simplicity and sometimes good design. This is true of hobo signs, which developed over hundreds of years. But we cannot wait, now, for signs to develop in this way. We do not have the time.

Designers study signs from the past, and use them when they can. They learn about how people react to certain designs. It has been found, for example, that people who cannot read have trouble understanding abstract signs and pictographs that have a symbolic meaning. They can interpret signs better if they have had some experience with letters and numbers. After all, these are abstract signs, too.

A system of signs will not be practical unless the separate signs can be combined to make other meanings. Otherwise, thousands of new signs would have to be made. We have seen how combinations were used in ancient sign systems, such as Egyptian hieroglyphs, and how they have been carefully planned in Semantography.

Signs are needed for many activities in our modern world. Perhaps the most obvious need is for signs to guide international travelers. The International Road Signs deal with only one kind of travel. Signs that can be understood by everyone are needed at airports, at world's fairs and exhibits, at railroad stations, museums, hotels, and other places visited by large numbers of people.

As we have seen, better signs are also needed for industry and science, for instructions on machines and other goods sent to foreign countries, for the work of engineers and mechanics.

Here is a partial list of the kinds of information that can be conveyed by graphic signs. Designers are already working on signs for this purpose.

airport	doctor
bus stop	do not touch
danger	don't drink this water

elevator	lunchroom
entrance	men's room
exit	no smoking
fragile	police
hospital	post office
hotel	railroad station
information	telephone
ladies' room	wet paint

A few of the items on this list are already covered by the International Road Signs. Most are not. We simply do not have adequate signs for this kind of information. Some international events, such as world exhibitions, have had signs of their own. A set of signs directing people to services was especially designed for the Tokyo Olympic Games of 1964. Here are some of these:

cloakroom

shower

lunchroom

dining room

telephone

First Aid

These are amusing signs. However, one criticism was that the designers should have made more use of existing signs, instead of producing entirely new ones. Some of these were also not clear in meaning. Why the design for cloakroom, for example? Would most people grasp the difference between lunchroom and dining room? Why not use the established international sign for telephone? And for First Aid? These are reasonable questions. Again, we can see how difficult it is to design effective signs for the future. But people at the Olympics did find their way around much better than they would have if all the signs had been in words.

At these same Olympic Games, signs were designed for identifying different sports. These were more successful.

How many of these can you identify? Of course, people watching the games could also refer to their programs, which were printed in a number of languages.

EXPO67, the Universal and International Exhibition of 1967, in Montreal, Canada, provided twenty-four signs without words for visitors from all over the world. Six of these follow.

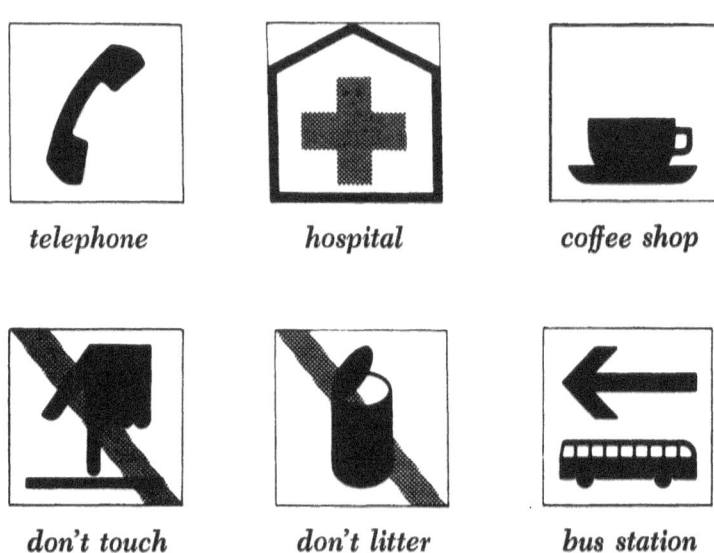

telephone   hospital   coffee shop

don't touch   don't litter   bus station

Let's look at these signs critically. The first three are easy for most people to understand. They served their purpose for fair-goers. The other three signs are more difficult. The "don't touch" sign is not clear. Why a hand pointing *down*?

A broad line across a sign, from corner to corner, evidently means "don't." But in the "don't litter" sign, does this line mean "Don't use the garbage can"? Surely that was not the intention.

What is the meaning of the arrow in the "bus station" sign? Does it point to a bus station (as it is meant to do) or to the direction in which the bus goes?

Perhaps none of these signs will ever be accepted for international use. Nevertheless, some of them are better than many signs we have now.

Suppose, for example, you are traveling in Yugoslavia. You

notice a door with a man's shoe painted on it. Does it mark a shoe-repair shop? A shoeshine place? Another door shows a lady's shoe with a high heel. What does *that* mean? In Yugoslavia, these signs mean "men's room" and "ladies' room." But how could *you* be expected to know that?

In our own country, a traveler from abroad might be just as puzzled at seeing, in a restaurant, a door with a man's hat pictured on it and another door with a woman's bonnet. Once he learned what these meant, the traveler would certainly be confused to find entirely different signs on the same little doors in other restaurants.

The present confusion of signs seems almost impossible to cope with. In general, it seems best to consider all the existing signs, with the possible exception of some of the International Road Signs, as experiments. They are steps on the way to developing acceptable signs for international use. More research is needed before the job can be considered finished. The trouble is that, once any signs are adopted, even for use in just a few places, they are difficult to change. Bad signs are as hard to change as good ones.

In spite of this fact, we will have to accept a certain number of makeshift signs for the time being. The need is so great that we cannot always wait for effective signs to be developed and accepted throughout the world. The process is too long and too slow. Most people today do not even know that such signs are needed. Very few organizations are aware of their importance.

Some temporary signs can be pictographs, especially when they are to be used only locally. But the pictographs must be up-to-date. Take, for example, signs explaining the use of a pay telephone. The telephone shown in the pictograph should be the model currently in use. Coins pictured should not be old ones.

ISOTYPE may prove useful as a starting point for new signs. The influence of ISOTYPE on signs in this country is already considerable. And some of the signs proposed for Semantography can be used.

A number of organizations are now working on signs for the future. We have seen how the United States of America Standards Institute works at developing signs for industry and engineering. The International Organization for Standardization in Geneva, Switzerland, does the same on a worldwide scale.

ICOGRADA, the International Council of Graphic Design Associations, helps organizations to cooperate with one another in the making of signs. A commission on international signs and symbols has been set up. The aim is to develop signs that are well designed and so clear that they can easily be learned by people everywhere. If organizations will work together, they can avoid the confusion of producing different signs for the same meaning.

Here are four signs from a student project sponsored by ICOGRADA. These are part of a set of twenty-four, which could form the basis for a complete system of signs. The two designers were students at Konstfackskolan, a school of

hotel

airport

information

doctor

design in Stockholm, Sweden. They won a Special Certificate of Merit. Notice the simplicity of the designs. The students felt that international signs should be so easy to reproduce that the people who use them could draw their own.

These are just one attempt at a solution to the problem of creating practical signs for the future. New signs will have to be tested all over the world before they can finally be adopted. One disadvantage of the above signs is their circular shape. That shape has already been accepted by the International Organization for Standardization as indicating a prohibition—*don't* do this or that.

Incidentally, the sign for "doctor" in the ICOGRADA set is also the hobo sign meaning "open eye—police looking for hoboes." Probably only hoboes would be confused by that!

There is a new word for signs and symbols that is also an old word—"glyphs." This is a part of the word "hieroglyph," which we have met before. "Glyph" comes from the Greek word *glyphein*, which means "carving." In the early days of man's history, many glyphs were carved in stone. Now signs are hardly ever carved, but the word "glyph" is a catchy one, and it seems likely that it is here to stay. Words have a way of changing their meaning as people use them.

Most of the signs and symbols in this book can be called glyphs, but today the word "glyphs" is used primarily to mean universally accepted signs and symbols. Perhaps this word can help clear up the confusion caused by the different meanings of the words "sign" and "symbol." If we take this definition of glyph seriously, we find that there are not really many now in use: numerals, letters, mathematical signs, musical signs, punctuation marks, scientific symbols. All of these have developed and been accepted over a period of many years. The International Road Signs were adopted more recently. These cannot as yet be considered true glyphs because they are not universally accepted. The day of glyphs as an effective aid to international understanding is still to come.

The United Nations considered glyphs so important for international communication that they were made a part of its program for the International Cooperation Year, in 1965. Member nations were encouraged to invent new signs that could become glyphs, and to agree on old ones. The United Nations had its own symbol for the International Cooperation Year:

Once glyphs are accepted for international use, UNESCO (The United Nations Educational, Scientific, and Cultural Organization) can help promote their use all over the world.

Try making some signs yourself. Begin with some of the familiar subjects we have shown here. Then see if your friends and neighbors can figure out the meaning of your signs—but remember that even the best of signs must be learned before their meaning is clear to everyone.

A sign is a small thing in this big world, hardly ever more than a foot or two across, more often small enough to be drawn or printed on an ordinary piece of paper. Yet signs and symbols have a big job to do. It is hard even to imagine how much they can contribute to better understanding among the peoples of the world.

Bibliography

BOOKS OF SPECIAL INTEREST TO YOUNG PEOPLE

GENERAL

"Art in Communications" (booklet). Denver, Colorado: Denver Art Museum, 1963.

BEARD, DANIEL. *The American Boy's Book of Signs, Signals, and Symbols*. Philadelphia: J.B. Lippincott Co., 1918. (Out of print)

EPSTEIN, SAM and BERYL. *The First Book of Codes and Ciphers*. New York: Franklin Watts, 1956.

KOCH, RUDOLPH. *The Book of Signs*. New York: Dover Publications, n.d.

LEHNER, ERNEST. *American Symbols, a Pictorial History*. New York: William Penn Publishing Corporation, 1957.

————. *The Picture Book of Symbols*. New York: William Penn Publishing Corporation, 1956.

"Shape and Form" (booklet). Denver, Colorado: Denver Art Museum, 1960.

ON WRITING, NUMERALS, AND SUCH

CAHN, WILLIAM and RHODA. *The Story of Writing, From Cave Art to Computer.* New York: Harvey House, 1963.

EPSTEIN, SAM and BERYL. *The First Book of Words.* New York: Franklin Watts, 1954.

FOLSOM, FRANKLIN. *The Language Book.* New York: Grosset and Dunlap, 1963.

HOFSINDE, ROBERT. *Indian Picture Writing.* New York: William Morrow and Co., 1959.

IRWIN, KEITH GORDON. *The Romance of Writing.* New York: The Viking Press, 1956.

LAUBER, PATRICIA. *The Story of Numbers.* New York: Random House, 1961.

OGG, OSCAR. *The 26 Letters.* New York: Thomas Y. Crowell, 1961.

SMITH, DAVID EUGENE, and JEKUTHIEL GINSBURG. *Numbers and Numerals* (booklet). Washington, D.C.: National Council of Teachers of Mathematics, 1937.

THOMPSON, TOMMY. *The A B C of Our Alphabet.* London and New York: Studio Publications, 1942.

TOMKINS, WILLIAM. *Universal American Indian Sign Language.* San Diego, California: privately printed, 1927.

ADULT BOOKS

ARNELL, ALVIN. *Standard Graphical Symbols.* New York: McGraw Hill Book Co., 1963.

Bliss, C.K., *Semantography (Blissymbolics).* Coogee, Sydney, Australia: Semantography (Blissymbolics) Publications, 1965. Distributed in the U.S. by Carol Cox Book Co., Paramus, New Jersey 07652.

CIRLOT, J. E. *A Dictionary of Symbols.* New York: Philosophical Library, 1962.

"Computers—Theory and Uses" (booklet). Washington, D.C.: National Science Teachers' Association, 1964.

Design Quarterly 62: "Signs and Symbols in Graphic Communication." Minneapolis: Walker Art Center, 1965.

DIRINGER, DAVID. *The Alphabet, a Key to the History of Mankind.* New York: Philosophical Library, 1948.

———. *Writing.* New York: Frederick A. Praeger, 1962.

GELB, I. J. *A Study of Writing.* Chicago: University of Chicago Press, 1952.

GOLDSMITH, ELISABETH E. *Ancient Pagan Symbols.* New York: G.P. Putnam's Sons, 1929.

———. *Sacred Symbols in Art.* New York: G.P. Putnam's Sons, 1912.

HAWKES, JACQUETTA. *Man and the Sun.* New York: Random House, 1962.

JUNG, CARL G., et al. *Man and His Symbols.* New York: Doubleday and Co., 1964.

KAMEKURA, YUSAKA. *Trademarks of the World.* New York: George Wittenborn, n.d.

KENTON, EDNA. *The Book of Earths.* New York: William Morrow and Co., 1928.

KEPES, GYORGY (ed.). *Sign, Image, Symbol.* New York: George Braziller, 1966.

MALLERY, GARRICK. *Picture-Writing of the American Indians.* Washington, D.C.: United States Bureau of American Ethnology, 10th Annual Report, 1888–89, 1893.

MASON, WILLIAM R. *A History of the Art of Writing.* New York: The Macmillan Co., 1920.

MUNARI, BRUNO. *Discovery of the Circle.* New York: George Wittenborn, n.d.

SCHOOLCRAFT, HENRY R. *Information Respecting the History, Condition, and Prospects of the Indian Tribes of the United States,* Vol. 1. Philadelphia: Lippincott, Gambo and Co., 1853.

WHITNEY, ELWOOD (ed.). *Symbology, the Use of Symbols in Visual Communications.* New York: Hastings House, 1960.

WILDBUR, PETER. *Trademarks.* London: Studio Vista; New York: Reinhold Publishing Co., 1966.

Index